Antoine Robidoux

and Fort Uncompahgre

The Story of a Western Colorado Fur Trader

Printed in the United States
10 9 8 7 6 5 4 3 2 1

Library of Congress Cataloging-in-Publication Data
Reyher, Ken
Antoine Robidoux and Fort Uncompahgre : the story of a western
Colorado fur trader / Ken Reyher

Includes bibliographical references and index

Library of Congress Catalog Card Number: 98-87114

ISBN 1-890437-13-1

Western Reflections, Inc.
PO Box 710 • Ouray, CO 81427

1998
First Edition

Front cover painting "Paradise", oil on canvas, copyright 1997 Dan
Deuter.

Book and cover design by Kathryn Retzler, Circle B Publications,
Ouray, Colorado.

Antoine Robidoux
and Fort Uncompahgre

The Story of a Western Colorado Fur Trader

By Ken Reyher

Western Reflections Inc.
Ouray, Colorado

The Author

Courtesy *San Juan Silver Stage*

Ken Reyher's family came to Colorado in the years that followed the Civil War. He grew up listening to stories from his grandfather Bill Reyher who, as a boy, had worked cattle with veterans of the Texas longhorn trails. Grandfather Henry Weimer, a former cavalryman, shared in the story telling. After a seven-year tour in the military, Reyher returned to Colorado where he taught high school history for twenty years, operated a flying service and engaged in farming. Stories about the early days of the state continue to play a role in his life. His articles about the old west have appeared in several magazines, and he writes regularly for two western Colorado newspapers, for one of which he is the history editor. This is his first book. ✦

Contents

Antoine Robidoux, 1843. At home in either the latest fashions of the day or the greasy buckskins of a mountain trapper, young Antoine Robidoux proved himself the master of both worlds. Within four years of first entering Santa Fe, he had become a Mexican citizen, was married to the governor's daughter and had been granted the right to control trade in what would someday become western Colorado and eastern Utah.

Courtesy Museum of New Mexico.

Preface

For Antoine Robidoux, Saint Louis had become too confining, too settled and too predictable. What had been a collection of log huts in his father's day had grown into a center of commerce and an open gate pointing toward the vast western frontier. That gate proved irresistible and in 1824 young Antoine headed his horse down the 800 mile trail towards Santa Fe and the newly independent nation of Mexico. He rode alongside American wagons loaded with trade goods and watched in the Santa Fe plaza as those goods were exchanged for Mexican silver. From Santa Fe he rode northwest into an unexplored wilderness. There he found streams teeming with beaver and mountain valleys inhabited by friendly bands of Ute Indians as eager for American trade goods as were the citizens of Santa Fe. More importantly he found a region still free from the tentacles of the powerful American fur companies headquartered back in St. Louis. Antoine returned to Santa Fe. Young, handsome, and gifted with both social graces and the Spanish language, he quickly became integrated into Santa Fe society, was granted Mexican citizenship and was elected to the city council. He courted and married the governor's daughter and obtained a trading license that gave him control over a territory covering what would one day become western Colorado and eastern Utah. In the years that followed he built three trading posts and an empire that successfully challenged even the powerful British Hudson Bay Company. Then, almost as quickly, Antoine's world came crashing down and one of the great chapters of the early west came to an end. ✦

Joseph Robidoux III. Seen here when he was about eighty, Robidoux saw to it that his five younger brothers always had a reliable link to both eastern fur markets and necessary trade goods. He founded the city of St. Joseph, Missouri and lived to see it rival St. Louis as a gateway to the west.
Courtesy Saint Joseph Historical Society.

Chapter 1
From Canada to Santa Fe

N orth America of the early 1700s was a forbidding place to the men and women who had established a tenuous hold on its eastern shores. English and other European settlers who lived from the Carolinas north to the New England colonies had long given up dreams of duplicating Spanish feats in Mexico. There was no gold or silver in the dark and brooding forests that lay westward toward what seemed like infinity. Instead, the colonists had learned their futures lay in the land itself: farming, livestock and timber for ships. Fleets were built for fishing and commerce. Further north along the banks of the St. Lawrence River, a different drama was beginning to play out.

For generations, rich and powerful men in Europe had favored felt hats made from beaver fur. Viewed under a microscope, each hair from the inner coat of this animal has tiny barbs extending outward along the shaft interlocking one hair with the next. This provides protection for the animal from cold water in the same manner that a wet suit protects a diver. It was discovered that felt made from beaver fur could be shaped into hats that were resistant to wet weather and able to retain their shape even after hard use. The demand for such hats decimated the European beaver population. This fact was not lost on the early French explorers who trekked through the wilderness of Eastern Canada. They found the creatures in abundance along with powerful tribes of native people willing to trade skins for steel knives, blankets and firearms. It was into this world that France began sending traders, storekeepers, farmers and craftsmen—nearly all dedicated to one purpose, acquisition of the rich, dark pelts of the beaver. So, a trading alliance was born.

It was during these years that the Robidoux family came to Canada to build a new life in the promising wilderness. As the years passed, family members moved further west and then south into the regions drained by the Mississippi River.

Joseph Robidoux II, born in Canada in 1750 and raised in the beaver trade, reached the already thriving village of St. Louis by the time he was twenty. French explorers had established the settlement in 1764 on the west bank of the Mississippi and just below the confluence with the Missouri. The primary purposes of the town were to serve as a collection point for beaver furs coming down the Missouri River and to provide support for traders venturing into its drainage regions. When young Robidoux arrived, the outpost had a population of no more than 400 whites and 200 slaves. With wealth flowing from upriver, St. Louis continued to grow. In 1810 the colony counted a permanent population of 1,400 and by 1820 the number had grown to nearly 5,000—a mixture of French, American, Spanish, German, Indians and Black slaves. Competition had become intense as large firms fought for control of the beaver trade and the fortunes it could provide.

Joseph Robidoux remained within the circle of independent French traders and spent twelve years building his own trading venture. Then, certain his road to success was assured, he married a French/American girl from Cahokia, Illinois. Catherine Rollet bore her husband nine children. Six sons spent the major portions of their lives involved in the fur trade and in the same manner as their father who helped open the Missouri trade, they pioneered yet another frontier—the American southwest. One son, Antoine, left his name associated with a vast trading empire that included what would one day become western Colorado and eastern Utah.

Following the early death of the boys' father, it was the eldest son, Joseph III, who took the reins of the family trading business. Respected, shrewd and a born leader, he became a father figure to his younger siblings and a spokesman for other French/American traders and trappers. Joseph maintained control of the family business until he was slowed by the infirmities of old age. His brothers, restless and venturesome, preferred the frontier rather than the counting house. At that point they were unaware that circumstance would soon take them far beyond the banks of the Mississippi.

Following Mexico's independence from Spain in 1821, the new government opened the southwest to American traders. Trade goods began moving from St. Louis westward, and growing quantities of Mexican silver returned east in rawhide bags. When it became evident the trade route would remain open, the Robidoux brothers wasted no time in making plans to go west.

In the spring of 1824, Antoine and his brother Louis rode 800 miles to Santa Fe where they made connections with an old family friend and close ally, Auguste Chouteau. As a fourteen-year-old boy, Chouteau had been among the original French settlers who helped establish St. Louis. He had watched it pass from French control to that of powerful fur companies backed by American money. Sensing new opportunity in the southwest, the aging Auguste and his son Pierre resettled in Santa Fe. Their presence opened the first of many doors for young Antoine and his brothers. Opportunity also came in the person of Etienne Provost, another family friend who had come to Santa Fe, partly with the financial backing of Joseph Robidoux. Late in the summer of 1824, Provost led a party of trappers, including Antoine, into the wilderness of what would become western Colorado and eastern Utah. It was their intention to explore potential new beaver country. What they found excited them: streams filled with beaver and nearby Ute Indians, friendly and eager to trade. The expedition continued north and near today's Wyoming border, Antoine and five companions separated from the main group and continued into present day southwest Wyoming. There, they were attacked by hostile Arapaho who had ventured far west of their own traditional range. One trapper was killed and the rest of Antoine's group was robbed of everything they had, right down to their underwear. Provost's men fared even worse. Forced into a fight with Shoshone warriors, nearly half his followers were killed. Antoine reconnected with Provost and the expedition returned to Taos in mid-winter of 1825. Although the trip had proven a disaster, both Antoine and Provost saw great potential in the region, particularly the lands occupied by the peaceful Utes. Provost returned the following three winters to trap and trade.

Antoine remained in the Santa Fe region long enough to realize that the southwest contained not only virgin streams rich with beaver, but that French traders had a definite advantage over Americans in regards to relations with both Mexican officials and local citizens. Although all traders were tolerated, cultural and religious differences formed a barrier between the often loud, impatient and Protestant Americans and their Catholic hosts who preferred doing business in a more contained manner. The French, on the other hand, had long ago learned to work within the confines of local custom and culture and they shared the same Catholic faith. With these thoughts in mind, Antoine and Louis returned east to a new trading post recently built by their brother Joseph. Located more than 200 miles up the Missouri River, this new establishment removed the family enterprises from the brawling competition of St. Louis. This new post eventually became the city of Saint Joseph, named after the Biblical saint, but its history would forever be linked to Joseph Robidoux III.

After a short stay at the new site, Antoine returned to Santa Fe, this time taking his brothers Isadore and Michel. Louis followed a few months later bringing the remaining brother, Francois.

In the few months they had been gone, Antoine and Louis discovered that Mexican officials had passed laws forbidding future American incursions into the regions west and north of Santa Fe. This included the very country Antoine and Provost had recently visited. Mexican trappers were already working the streams of Arizona and the

American, British, French and Mexican trappers who plied the streams of the western wilderness often lived between two cultures. Their tools and methods reflected their European heritage, but their daily lives more closely mirrored the practical aspects of local Indian life.

Courtesy *Delta County Independent*

lighter colored fur they brought in sold for a premium over the darker beaver found further north. Santa Fe officials feared that if Americans were allowed to trap, they would take their furs and bypass Santa Fe on their way back to American territory. Government officials had no intention of losing tax revenues. But there was a solution. French trappers were being allowed into the interior provided they become Mexican citizens. Antoine and his brother Louis quickly filed the necessary paperwork. The fact they were Roman Catholic satisfied one condition. Being gainfully employed was the second requirement, so they opened a trading house near the town square. They needed only to wait out a twenty-four month probationary period. Citizenship would also give them an advantage that itinerant traders did not have—they would be taxed at a much lower rate on their goods and furs. While the probationary period ran its course, the two brothers began to integrate themselves into Santa Fe society.

Antoine, in particular, was a charmer. Equally at home in the wilderness or the best homes of Santa Fe, and gifted in his ability with the Spanish language, he quickly became an accepted part of the town's social elite—so much so that in 1827, he was elected to the Santa Fe City Council. Antoine began his political career by taking a stand against American traders and trappers attempting to flaunt local laws. Eager to enter into business deals which showed promise of profit, he engaged in trading trips south into Chihuahua and Sonora. To finance the trips Antoine borrowed money from his Santa Fe friends using furs stored in the brothers' Santa Fe warehouse as collateral. In 1828 he invested heavily in a gold mine near Taos. When it failed, he settled his debts without complaint. This act gained him great favor among his new Mexican friends and creditors. Although the mine was a disappointment, other aspects of Antoine's life were not.

For some time, he had been courting the Mexican governor's adopted daughter. Carmel Benevides had been taken under the governor's protection following the death of her father, a career army officer. Vivacious and with an unusual sense of daring, the sixteen-year-old beauty thought nothing of riding fifty miles on horseback to Albuquerque with friends and dancing until dawn. On one occasion she swam her horse across the flooding Rio Grande River and then dared her male escorts to follow. They refused. Perhaps it was such traits that attracted the attention of the young French/American.

Don Antoine Robidoux received the governor's permission to marry Carmel in 1828. It proved to be a good union. As the son-in-law of Santa Fe's most powerful official, doors opened for Antoine that might otherwise have remained closed. Within weeks he received what amounted to an exclusive license to trade and trap in what would some-day become western Colorado and eastern Utah. Antoine had already proven loyal to Mexico by his stand against American trappers work-ing in Mexican territory. Such feelings had come from animosity that had been building for two generations. From the time of Antoine's father, the Robidoux family had fought for a share of the Missouri River trade against powerful competitors. One—the American Fur Com-pany—had already entered the Uintah Basin of eastern Utah by the middle 1820s. The company was confident Santa Fe was too far away to do much about it. It is possible Mexican authorities saw a potential foil in young Robidoux who gave every indication of fully supporting his new government. ✦

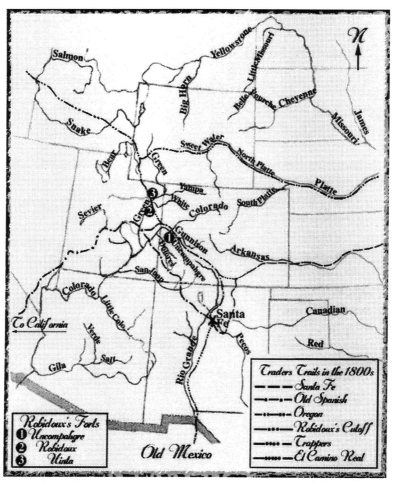

The opening of the American southwest was made possible by a series of trails developed over more than two centuries. These routes formed the commercial link between the Pacific coast, the eastern United States and Mexico.

Chapter 2
Roads of Commerce

Antoine's future in the Southwest depended on a system of trails that connected New Mexico with not only Saint Louis and points east but Mexico City and the California settlements. Santa Fe lay at the northern end of *El Camino Real* (The Royal Road). It was a route laid out by Juan de Onate in 1598 over what probably had been an ancient system of Indian trails. Stretching from Mexico City to Santa Fe, this track covered 1,800 torturous miles and passed through some of the driest deserts in North America. It took up to five months of sustained travel for cart or pack train caravans to reach the northern terminus. Trade caravans generally came north from the capital once every three years. As a result, few goods other than what was most essential found their way to Mexico's northernmost towns. By 1800 that began to change.

Ranchers of the Rio Grande Valley were producing a growing surplus of sheep which they drove south over the trail—600 miles to silver rich but meat poor Chihuahua—and traded for silver coin and bullion. With very few mines of their own, the people of the Santa Fe region had, up to that point, operated primarily on a barter system. With the Chihuahua trade established, silver became plentiful in the Rio Grande Valley. In addition to coins and bars, the white metal was used to lavishly decorate saddles and bridles. Most households of consequence possessed a variety of silver housewares and personal items.

Large flocks of sheep produced surplus wool. The industrious New Mexicans began spinning it into yarn. Soon nearly every household owned a loom with which blankets could be made. To expand the craft, master weavers were brought up from southern Mexico to teach new color techniques and weaving designs. The Chihuahua trade expanded further with this new product. Shortly after 1810, a handful of venturesome traders discovered that fellow countrymen living along the California coast were willing to trade horses and mules for Santa Fe blankets although few caravans were willing to attempt the dangerous trek across Arizona. In addition to problems regarding difficult terrain and hostile Indians, water and forage were in perpetual short supply. Traders wanted a more reliable trail, hopefully free of hostile Indians. This brought an additional problem because officials in far away Mexico City had proven hesitant to allow expansion beyond the regions that could be patrolled by local garrison troops.

Over the years, northern colonists had developed a sense of independence from official policy, and the first traders who made the trip to California had proven that the coastal market could be profitable. Government policy or not, Mexican entrepreneurs became determined to find a better trail than the one across Arizona. An attempt to open a reliable road to California had been made as early as 1776 when Fathers Francisco Dominguez and Silvestre Escalante and eight followers rode into what would become southwestern Colorado and eastern Utah. They reached present-day central Utah before turning back. In the half-century that followed, small parties of New Mexicans worked their way north and west, searching for gold and trading with local Indians. Little by little they progressed into the interior and in so doing, found a route to the coast that contained dependable supplies of forage, water and peaceful Indians.

By the early 1820s the trail was in active use. Known to history both as the Old Spanish Trail and The California Trail, it extended northwest out of Santa Fe, passed through southwestern Colorado, extended northwest into central Utah then southwest again until it reached Los Angeles. Travelers could count on a two month journey with pack animals. Even the rugged two wheeled carts that traveled *El Camino Real* could not negotiate the rugged terrain this route encountered crossing the western mountains.

Inhabitants of Santa Fe had come to depend on *El Camino Real* to market their primary product—sheep. While New Mexico was suitable for producing these browsing animals, pastures necessary to raise horses and mules were in short supply. As a result the California Trail soon became important as a conduit to exchange horses and mules raised in the verdant pastures of the coastal region for blankets woven in the Rio Grande Valley.

Most important to the Santa Fe area was the opening of the Santa Fe Trail by William Becknell in 1821. The route began in the Missouri settlements and angled southwest across Kansas where it intersected the Arkansas River. Holding the river in sight, the trail came west into Colorado then climbed over Raton Pass into New Mexico and finally

Trappers, traders and Indians traveled to Robidoux's fort where they could trade, resupply and continue their journey over one of the main trails between the east and California.

Courtesy *Delta County Independent*

west across the mountains to Santa Fe. Unlike the torturous trails leading to Mexico City and California, this newest route extended roughly
800 miles over mostly level territory that could be counted on to provide both water and forage during all but the coldest winter months.
More importantly, it provided a link between cash poor American manufacturers eager to exchange their products with Mexican citizens who
could pay in silver. In addition to returning with coin and bullion, the
freighters filled their wagons with Mexican blankets, beaver pelts from
trappers and tanned buffalo robes from Indian hunters. Although these
items were bulky and relatively low value compared to manufactured
goods, they helped add to the freighters' profits. It was this return journey that was of vital importance to the plans of Antoine Robidoux. He
needed inexpensive cargo space and the freighters could provide it.

Although *El Camino Real* gave birth to Santa Fe, its 1,800 mile
length made it impractical to adequately supply the northern colonies.
The Santa Fe Trail, 1,000 miles shorter and over terrain that could be
traversed throughout much of the year, soon became the lifeline of the
southwest. Teamsters needed a continuing supply of mules to pull the
heavy freight wagons that could be moved over the California Trail to
the waiting markets in Santa Fe. By 1828, when Antoine Robidoux
received his trading license, this system of trails was active and thriving.
It wasn't long before he began to add his own signature to these roads
of commerce.

Instead of following the established California Trail south around
the San Juan Mountains then north into Utah, Antoine took his pack
animals north out of Taos, traveled into the San Luis Valley of southern Colorado and then took an old Indian track over the continental
divide at Cochetopa Pass. From there he descended down into the Gunnison Valley, passed south of what is now Blue Mesa Reservoir, crossed
Cerro Summit and dropped into the Uncompahgre Valley where he
built his first trading post. This route became known as the Mountain
Branch of the California Trail. It is possible, according to some
accounts, that he might have sometimes used carts or wagons to the

top of Cochetopa Pass and possibly as far as the Gunnison Valley, where they were left and picked up again on the return trip. But in the region south of Blue Mesa Reservoir, pack animals were the vehicles of choice. Robidoux himself referred to that section as the "son-of-a-bitch" portion of the trail. His description was borne out in 1853 when Major John Gunnison for the first time traversed the route with wagons. His

men spent days digging and filling, moving boulders, cutting trees and even raising and lowering vehicles with block and tackle up and down cliffs in order to cross this region. But for Antoine, the north route was shorter and could be relied on to provide better forage and water than the main trail south and west of the San Juan Mountains. Because of trade caravans and horse herds returning from California, the southern portion of the trail was often short of grass and water. Even so, winter weather

Travel on the early western trails was seldom without dangers and hardships.
Courtesy Dan Dueter

closed the northern branch and then the only option was to take the southern route.

After his trading posts were established, Antoine opened a track that branched off from the Santa Fe Trail in southern Colorado and passed near present day Pueblo. From there it wound around the south end of the Wet Mountains and crossed Mosca Pass before dropping down into the southern extremities of the Great Sand Dunes. From that point, the path traversed across the San Luis Valley until it intersected the trail going up Cochetopa Pass. Rugged and difficult, the route was shorter than following the primary trail to Santa Fe, and perhaps more importantly, goods brought in over this cutoff did not have to pass through the hands of government customs agents.

In addition, Antoine's presence in western Colorado opened yet another route across the west. Trappers, traders and others began traveling southeast out of Idaho to reach his forts where they could trade, resupply and continue their journey down to Santa Fe over the California Trail. The Idaho route became a branch of the Trappers Trail. British employees of the Hudson Bay Company also began making use of this trail as they edged ever closer to Mexican territory.

In 1828, the Southwest was a vast, rugged land sandwiched between Mexico's colonies in the Rio Grande Valley and the coastal regions of California. Until Antoine, there had been almost no official presence in the remote interior. Four years earlier, an American Fur Company brigade had entered the Uintah Basin to trap under the leadership of famed mountain man, Jedediah Smith, who was so impressed with the region that his employer, William Ashley, took a party and explored as far south as Vernal, Utah. Despite abundant beaver and friendly Indians, Utah stretched the limits in terms of distance and supply, so the Americans pulled back into Wyoming. It is probable that Mexican officials knew about these probes into their territory. However, more than 400 miles of rugged mountains were between them and the trespassers so there was little they could do about it except grant young Antoine the authority to deal with future trespassers under the auspices of Mexican law—enforced frontier style if necessary. All that would wait, however until Antoine first established himself with the Ute Indians who controlled the region.

An issue of extreme importance was exactly where to build his trading post. It is likely that question was answered in three ways: Antoine was familiar with the Uncompahgre Valley in western Colorado; logistics dictated that a trading post be within easy reach of the

California Trail; and, very likely he received advice from the Ute people who inhabited the area.

It was common to locate trading posts at or near the confluence of two rivers. In the trackless lands of the west, travelers frequently followed streams. The juncture where two rivers came together could be located more easily, an important point for potential customers unfamiliar with a region. In addition, timber and grazing ground covered a far bigger acreage near a western river confluence. Because of this fact, native Americans used these areas to camp and graze their horse herds, particularly during the winter months. For these reasons, Antoine selected a site two miles below the confluence of the Gunnison and Uncompahgre Rivers, convenient also because it was a short distance from a natural fording place. Rich in timber and grass, the area was downstream from a favored Ute gathering place just above the confluence. A huge living cottonwood—already good size in Robidoux's

Fort buildings were simple log structures chinked with adobe mud. The roof consisted of poles and willow branches with almost a foot of dirt on top. Rooms were small and most employees slept crowded together on the dirt floor.

Ken Reyher photo

With little more than an adobe and mud forge and simple hand tools, an early western blacksmith did everything from shoe horses and mules to make major repairs on wagons. He could also repair rifles, fabricate tools and was often a skilled carpenter.

Courtesy *Delta County Independent*

day and known as the Ute Council Tree—still stands on the site of this old campground. This particular location was known for its easy winters, was free from excessive wind and deep snow, and could be reached by the southern route of the California Trail. An additional bonus was that the valley was in the heart of Ute territory. A trading post in the center of their lands would relieve them of the 300 mile journey to Santa Fe where they had been going to trade.

The Utes also wanted a trader in their midst for a more sensitive reason. Spanish and Mexican law had prohibited the sale and trade of firearms to Indians. By 1825, substantial numbers of English muskets could be found in the hands of tribes living beyond the northern boundaries of Ute territory. Traders for the Hudson Bay Company out of Canada had found that a ten dollar musket could be exchanged for as much as $700 worth of beaver pelts. Unfortunately, the introduction of these weapons upset an already tenuous balance of power among some of the western tribes. The Utes had no intention of letting that happen if they could find the means to arm themselves. Perhaps, far from the prying eyes of Santa Fe, they might convince the new trader to provide them with guns as well as knives, kettles and blankets.

Fort Uncompahgre was constructed in 1828, and Antoine conducted his first trades that same year. Other than the fact that the fort was built on the south bank of the Gunnison River, little is known about its size or physical appearance. The fact that it was located in the heart of some of the most rugged country in the west made it unattractive to visit by the more literate travelers of that day. Consequently, very little was written about it. No account is known to exist that describes the actual structure, but it was probably an unpretentious post consisting of little more than a few crude log buildings surrounded by a fence of cottonwood pickets designed more to keep the livestock in at night rather than to keep potential enemies out. This is entirely logical because Antoine had nothing to fear from the Utes. The Indians he had to concern himself with were to the north. Even though they had firearms, the chance of Shoshone warriors attempting to venture deep into the Ute's mountain stronghold was almost nonexistent. Although seldom aggressive beyond their own borders, Ute warriors had a fierce reputation for protecting their lands.

Antoine might have had another reason for not wanting to invest in a substantial building program. Although the Utes were friendly, they had a long standing aversion for permanent structures built on tribal ground. Mexican settlers who ventured into the southern fringes of Colorado in the hopes of establishing new farms and ranches were nearly always chased out and their buildings torn down and destroyed. The practice of burning out squatters continued into the future, until the Utes were forced out of Colorado in the early 1880s.

Outside labor was needed to construct the post and to maintain its day-to-day functions. Accounts of the time indicate that from fifteen to eighteen employees worked at the fort. In addition to the individuals who handled trading affairs and did a limited amount of trapping, labor was required to package pelts and hides, care for the livestock and continue various construction projects. Pickets buried in the wet ground generally rotted off in three years, and chinking that had fallen out of the log walls of the buildings had to be replaced. It is possible as time passed, that at least part of the post might have been reconstructed from adobe. Antoine's employees were nearly all young Mexican men who were familiar with this style of building. With adobe bluffs little more than a rifle shot away, adequate material would have been available. It is also accepted that the post would have produced its own food. Land along the Gunnison River was similar to that along the Rio Grande. Although irrigation would have been necessary, the New Mexicans were adept at digging ditches and building elaborate watering systems.

Although no accounts exist as to what was grown at the post, it is likely that nearly anything raised in the Santa Fe area could have been produced in the fertile river bottom soils along the Gunnison. The Rio Grande Valley in New Mexico boasted staples such as corn, wheat, oats and beans, lentils, cabbage, potatoes, melons, and varieties of winter squash. Robidoux's employees probably planted fruit trees common in New Mexico. (Seventy-five years later, the region along the Gunnison became known nationwide for its orchards.) Milk cows and goats were kept. Workers harvested grass hay along the river and preserved it for winter use. This practice was important not only for the fort's domestic stock but for the pack animals used to bring supplies in and carry furs and pelts out. At least one cart or wagon would have been required to haul in the large quantities of firewood needed for heating and cooking.

Employees, brought up from Taos and the Santa Fe region, were customarily under a one year contract. They were paid in trade goods, most of which they received at the end of their service. There would have been little need for money at the fort. In Santa Fe at the time, skilled craftsmen made upwards of five dollars a month and field laborers no more than two dollars for the same amount of time. If a woman worked outside the home, she could expect no more than fifty cents to perhaps two dollars per month. With a surplus of labor in New Mexico and few job opportunities, it is doubtful that Robidoux had difficulty finding men willing to spend a year away from their homes even in the heart of Ute country. It is believed that, at least in the early years of post, one of the supervisory personnel brought his wife to serve as fort cook. She would have had a female assistant. Two meals were served each day, one at mid-morning and a second in late afternoon.

Conditions at the fort were Spartan at best. Guests furnished their own bedrolls and slept on the hard packed adobe floor. The chief clerk, generally a man with writing and accounting skills, ranked a small room of his own with a bed and a writing table.
Courtesy *Delta County Independent*

Quarters for general laborers would have consisted of little more than a place to spread their bedroll on the floor at night. In addition to shelter for the workers, the post would have designated at least one room for the cook. It would have contained a specially built fireplace designed so that hot coals could be raked towards the front upon which skillets and other vessels could be placed. Cooking utensils were not that much different from today with the exception of a large, flat sheet of iron with a handle on one end. The *comal*, as it was called, was used to bake *tortillas—* the flat, pancake-like staple of southwest cooking. Bread would also have been available, made very similarly to bread today and baked in an outside adobe oven shaped like an old-fashioned beehive. The cook and her husband would have used the kitchen as their own sleeping quarters. A second nearby room would have been available to store meat and food staples.

Frontier trading posts contained a special building in which to store trade items. It would have been windowless, with a heavy door and probably a lock. Nearby would have been a room to store hides and furs. Windowless and used principally to protect pelts prior to shipment, it also sheltered surplus trade goods, tack, saddles and other items that needed to be kept out of the weather. A separate building would have been available for visiting travelers, particularly trappers and mountain men. Conditions were Spartan at best. Guests furnished their own bedrolls and slept on the hard-packed adobe floor. The chief clerk, generally a man with writing and accounting skills, ranked a small room of his own with a bed and a writing table.

The primary building on the post would have been the trade room. It was there that both whites and Indians brought their furs, to be graded for quality and then weighed on a simple beam scale. Afterwards, depending on condition and weight, customers selected from a variety of items stocked on the shelves behind the counter. Quarters for the trading post owner or his representative often adjoined the trade room— both for convenience and security. Most posts, Fort Uncompahgre included, employed the services of a blacksmith who often doubled as fort carpenter. Mules and horses needed to be shoed, pack saddles kept serviceable, traps repaired, knives and axes sharpened. Most blacksmiths made minor repairs and fabrications for trappers, fort personal, local Indians and anyone passing through.

Although Antoine employed Mexican trappers and mountain men, he relied heavily on trade with the Ute Indians. The Tabaguache band claimed the same valley where he had built his fort. The area south of the San Juan Mountains was home to the Moache group, and the Capote band lived east of them. The latter often hunted and camped in the San

Luis Valley. The Yampa and White River Utes (also called the Grand River band) lived in what would become northwestern Colorado, while the Weeminuche group roamed in the regions west of the Colorado Continental Divide. The seventh band of Ute people were the Laguna or Uintah Utes who claimed the lands southeast of Great Salt Lake. Antoine, like his French ancestors before him, knew that Indians would willingly trap on their own lands and provide steady commerce with the local trader. Few Native Americans tolerated brigades of outside trappers who would come in, strip the streams of beaver and then leave. Contrary to popular history, many Native American tribes caught on quickly to the economic possibilities of becoming participants in the western fur trade. ✦

Although Fort Uncompahgre did take in furs from small groups of American trappers operating in the western regions, its primary customers were people from the seven Ute bands that inhabited the valleys of western Colorado and the Great Basin of eastern Utah.

Courtesy *Delta County Independent*

Chapter 3
Traders and Trade Goods

Virgin streams and friendly Utes would hopefully translate into profits for Antoine and his brothers. Although frontier traders had substantial opportunities to make fortunes, they were equally exposed to big risks. The hope of reducing risk was one reason the Robidoux family chose to focus on the southwest. In the Missouri trade, large and powerful fur companies, often backed by eastern money, did not take lightly the smaller competitors who had a hand in the business. Profits increased with volume and the big companies did all they could to see that they acquired the majority of furs being brought in from the western regions. Often it meant putting pressure on smaller competitors. Buy-outs were common and when that did not work, more direct forms of persuasion were sometimes used. Sabotage, threats of personal or property damage and, in some cases, even Indian depredations, resulted—directed by one competitor against another.

During the 1820s a trapper could make from $150–$250 in as little as two weeks. A laborer in the eastern settlements would have to work an entire year for the same amount. Traders made even more and owners of the major fur companies often made huge fortunes in a few seasons, sold out and retired in comfort or used their wealth as springboards into other enterprises.

While the big fur companies engaged in heated and sometimes violent competition for both the upper Missouri and northern Rocky Mountain region, the Robidouxs had watched closely as traders cut the first ruts of the Santa Fe Trail. In 1824, $35,000 worth of goods made the trip. A year later that figure increased to $65,000 and it continued to grow. The big freight wagons were able to move goods at far less cost than pack animals or carts. They also returned to Missouri with their cargo beds partly empty. As mentioned earlier, Antoine, already having made his first trip though the beaver rich country west of the Continental Divide, realized that with this opportunity freighting costs from Santa Fe to St. Joseph could be substantially reduced. In addition, he had the option of having goods shipped west by his brother or he could purchase them from other suppliers who worked through the Santa Fe trading houses.

In the case of the latter, he chose to deal primarily with a recent immigrant from Spain, Manuel Alvarez, who had opened a trading store in Santa Fe. Bright, well educated and willing to deal with Americans when others of the Santa Fe community were hesitant, Alvarez built a successful operation which included business with Antoine and his brothers, particularly Louis and Francois. Loyal and accommodating towards his American friends, Alvarez later served as American Consul at Santa Fe, became an American citizen and eventually served as New Mexico's territorial lieutenant governor.

By dealing directly with Alvarez, Antoine avoided many of the problems faced by other American traders. Graft and bribery were rampant features within the Mexican customs system. To the outsider, unfair tariffs and taxes could seriously erode profits. For local businessmen and established citizens, the problem was minimal. Alvarez, as a local trader, was able to purchase Antoine's furs and deal directly with the freighters returning to the east. Since Antoine and his brothers spent much of their time away from Santa Fe, the relationship provided a reliable link to the eastern settlements.

Trade goods came directly to Santa Fe from the family warehouses in Missouri. Joseph helped supply his brothers as well as other traders in the region. This was in addition to his thriving Missouri trade. He had a distinct dislike for dealing with Americans and when possible preferred to work within the French/American community. On at least one occasion he purchased more than $3,500 worth of cloth, knives, hatchets, tobacco, vermillion, lead, sugar, and other supplies from Jean Laffite, the infamous pirate who helped Andrew Jackson save New Orleans from the British in 1814.

Once received in the company warehouses in Saint Joseph, items marked for Santa Fe had to be repackaged into retail quantities. When possible, heavy brown paper secured with string was the preferred shipping medium since objects were packed tightly one against the other in wagon beds that rode directly on the running gear. This feature resulted in the cargo being subjected to nearly 1,000 hours of abrasion and movement as the freighters bounced and jolted their way to Santa Fe. To restrict cargo damage, wagon beds were made to slant inward near the bottom and ends so that a load, when it settled, would compact even further. This feature, similar to that of a boat hull, helped give rise to the term "prairie schooner".

When Antoine picked up or purchased supplies in Santa Fe, they had to be loaded onto mules for a 300 mile trip over the mountains. Again, great care had to be taken to avoid damage as the pack animals worked their way through the terrain. They sometimes fell or brushed up against trees and rocks, all of which could potentially damage a pack's contents. Depending on size, each mule could carry from 200-300 pounds. During one of the few recorded trips, Antoine moved one ton of trade goods from Santa Fe to northeastern Utah. Considering the size of his operation and the number of employees, that might be considered average. For bulky items, freighting costs increased as additional animals and handlers were needed. Antoine's supply caravans were most active from early summer to late fall. If winter travel was necessary, he sent his mules west of Taos around the San Juan Mountains on the south branch of the California Trail and then north.

Once the trade goods reached their destination, they were marked up as much as two-and-one-half times the Santa Fe price. While this might seem extreme, records indicate Antoine's prices were in line with or slightly lower than those of other traders operating further north in American and British territory. A one-pound bar of bullet lead, for example, sold in St. Louis for sixteen to twenty cents. After being delivered to Santa Fe the value expanded to roughly forty cents. Wilderness traders further increased markup to $1.50. It must also be remembered that part of the increase went to pay Mexican customs which levied three percent of New Mexico prices in 1824. This climbed to twenty percent by 1839.

Antoine apparently gave fair prices for the furs and pelts he acquired. Not only did he service most of the Ute trappers and hunters in western Colorado and eastern Utah, but Anglo and Mexican trappers often traveled considerable distances to do their own trading at Fort Uncompahgre. Mountain men Kit Carson and Joe Walker dealt with Antoine numerous times. In one instance, Walker and his party, trapping in Arizona, came north to sell their pelts at the fort rather than make the only slightly longer journey east to Santa Fe.

Prices for trade goods remained almost constant during the 1820s and '30s. More and more wagons traveled the Santa Fe Trail; but when the New Mexico market became saturated, freighters turned their wagons south along the Rio Grande River towards El Paso and then deep into Mexico along *El Camino Real*. After selling their goods for Mexican silver, the caravans returned north carrying Mexican cottons, woolens, and exotics such as cocoa beans—which quickly gained a following in Santa Fe and Taos. The beans were roasted, ground into flour and added to hot water and mixed with sugar and vanilla. Even the Indians took a liking to hot chocolate. Raisins and other dried fruits that had been picked up in El Paso were resold in Santa Fe. These, too, found a place in the Indian trade. By the early 1830s, in addition to trade goods out of St. Louis and Saint Joseph, Fort Uncompahgre was stocking Mexican blankets, cocoa, spices and raisins. Occasionally, Antoine purchased goods from the British Hudson Bay Company operating out of southeastern Idaho.

During the 1820s, a western trapper could expect to receive from five to six dollars a pound for his beaver pelts, with each cleaned and dried hide weighing an average of one and a half pounds. Considering that an eastern laborer might work an entire month for the same money, it is easy to see why the western regions exerted such a strong pull on the men who chose to go west. However, beyond gross receipts there were often considerable expenses. Pelts taken in trade out west had

Fort Uncompahgre's trading inventory included coffee, tea, sugar, tobacco, metal implements, iron arrowheads and cooking pots, calico dress fabric, blankets and blanketing material, silks, lace, finished clothing, bandanas and silk scarves.
Courtesy *Delta County Independent*

to be transported all the way back to St. Louis or other frontier collection points. Transportation costs, depending on distance, could be expected to run from fifty cents to as much as $1.12 per pound of pelts. That price seems high, but it must be remembered that furs often had to be transported part of the distance on the backs of pack animals and because of their bulk, averaged 190 pounds per horse or mule.

Trappers generally sold or traded their pelts to fur consortiums which sent caravans of trade goods west each spring to arrive in time for the early summer rendezvous. But moving goods by pack train to the western mountains was expensive. Packers had to be hired, at premium wages, for a trip that commonly took five months from beginning to end. In addition, there was the risk factor. River crossings sometimes proved disastrous, goods could be easily damaged if not properly packed, and trains had to be heavily armed and of considerable size to discourage raids by hostile western tribes. Once trade goods reached the western mountains, they brought two or three times their St. Louis prices. Although the rendezvous procedure worked, it involved coordination between the traders and trappers in terms of both being at the same location during the same two or three week period during early summer. The system was abandoned a few years after the price of beaver pelts collapsed, but by that time a growing number of permanent trading posts had sprung up across the west.

Although Fort Uncompahgre did take in furs from small groups of American trappers operating in the western regions, its primary customers were people from the seven Ute bands that inhabited the valleys of western Colorado and the Great Basin of eastern Utah. The southern Utes had been trading in and out of the Santa Fe region long before Antoine Robidoux entered the scene. A limited amount of trade goods had reached the northern Utes as early as 1776, but even by 1825 such commerce was still limited. Eager for anything that might come from Santa Fe, these people willingly traded their furs for whatever they could acquire, including bags of raw coffee beans which, for a while anyway, were cooked and eaten. Once Fort Uncompahgre was open for business, tastes for trade goods became more sophisticated and special orders were often requested from eastern suppliers.

The first items of interest were those which could lift the Ute people out of the Stone Age and into that of iron. Common steel butcher knives were equally important with Ute men and women since both were involved in skinning and processing the animals they killed. Most popular were blades etched with the Green River insignia but any wooden handled butcher knife was acceptable. Most came with blades ranging from five to seven inches long and the new owner had to provide his or her own sheath. The trade axe followed the knife in importance. It was a small, hatchet used both for camp chores and splitting open large animal carcasses. Contrary to popular beliefs today, the tomahawk, as we know it, was seldom used as a weapon of war by the western tribes. To Ute women, long familiar with the difficulties of wilderness living, a steel knife and a hand axe made their work many times easier. In some accounts from the time, the latter tool was even referred to as a woman's ax. Additional items made from metal included copper cooking pots and sheet metal cooking containers similar to small buckets each with its own heavy wire handle. To prevent rusting during shipment, they were coated with a layer of oil and gums. This finish was baked on and it proved quite durable. Several sizes were made, each designed to nest one inside the other to save space. Fire steels were available and in heavy demand. When struck against a piece of flint, they produced a shower of white hot sparks that made fire starting a simple and rapid process.

The Ute men immediately took to iron arrow heads. Little more than flat pieces of metal made into the shape of projectile points, each needed to be given final shape and sharpened. For that, steel files were available and in sizes and types commonly found in hardware stores today. As time passed, warriors discovered that by obtaining the metal bands from wooden barrels, they could bypass the trader and cut their own iron arrowheads. Indian trappers also needed steel beaver traps and these sold at a premium.

Not only did metal implements make life easier, but they allowed individuals to become more productive in terms of the number of pelts and skins that could be acquired and processed. Beaver were plentiful, requiring only the tools and labor to take them. An industrious Ute warrior and his wife soon learned that there were other desirable things to be had at the trading post. High on the list were blankets and cloth. Although Ute women continued to make wide use of animals skins for clothing and cold weather gear, cloth quickly became popular. Robidoux's supply manifest for 1830 shows a total of 456 yards of cotton material ordered, the only type identified being corduroy. It is likely that the remainder included printed calicoes and other printed cotton as well as bleached, brown and blue cotton from Mexico, some of which came in twills, stripes and checks. Brown and blue striped denim was available from eastern sources. Robidoux's cloth order also included fifty-four yards of silk fabric and fifty-seven yards of lace binding.

In step with women of other western tribes at the time, Ute ladies preferred printed calicoes to come with round, square, diamond or

oblong patterns no more than a quarter inch across. Leaf and vine patterns were also popular. Favorite colors were red, black and purple. Unacceptable colors included yellow, orange, buff, light blue and pea green. Colors and patterns were important and on occasion, suppliers and traders found themselves holding inventories of cloth they could not even give away. Indian customers also expected calicoes to arrive in the same glossy, starched condition in which they had left the

Chinese merchants pressed green tea leaves into decorated blocks which traders could cut each block into smaller pieces. Sugar cones (right of the tea block) were rock hard for transport purposes. Leaf tobacco usually came in round packages tightly bound with light-weight rope which was in almost as much demand as the tobacco it protected.

Ken Reyher photo

factory. This often proved a challenge for packers who carried the bolts of cloth hundreds of miles on the backs of pack mules and in all kinds of weather.

Trading posts also carried Chinese scissors. Short and stubby with large handles, these tools gave Indian women the ability to produce clothing as complex and detailed as any available during that time. Ceremonial buckskin garments became works of art. With scissors came sewing needles that ranged in sizes still used today—numbers one through twelve. These came in brown paper packages, twenty five needles per package. Heavy glover's needles and sail needles were available as were metal awls. These latter items were used to punch holes in leather. Most Indian horsemen used saddles and tack they manufactured themselves.

Thread was made from linen, the most common was an unbleached brown product which came in coiled hanks and sold by the pound. A finer bleached linen thread was available in one and two ounce balls. Although cotton thread was used in the East as early as 1809, it did not appear in the West in appreciable quantities until about 1850.

Next on the inventory at Fort Uncompahgre, and surpassing cloth in terms of quantity, was blanketing material. Although finished blankets were available at the trading post, most sales involved bolts of material straight from the eastern mills. Depending on weight and value, rolls came in lengths of about thirty yards with width approximating standard blanket sizes today. In 1830, Robidoux shipped in over 960 yards. Unlike cloth inventories, which were generally specific as to type; blanket-

Traders often took their wares on the trail to the Indian camps. Items for trade were laid out on furs or blankets. Beads, knives, tomahawks, tobacco twists, firearms and gunpowder, in kegs bound by split willow hoops, were usually available.

Ken Reyher photo

ing was seldom identified by color or kind on the trade manifests. Most of it was made from wool. Red and green were popular colors, but it is likely that the majority came in unbleached, natural colors. One reason for stocking uncut bolts was that a good portion went for winter clothing and coats. Women were able to purchase the amount they needed rather than cut up an expensive, finished blanket and be left with the excess. Where blankets were used for sleeping purposes, it was common to purchase enough material to make one very long blanket. By making the proper folds, a sleeper could produce a satisfactory sleeping bag with a solid bottom.

Finished blankets were available and did sell at the trading post. The majority came from local looms in and around Santa Fe. Made from the long wool of the local Churro sheep, they were unbleached and designed for rugged use. Mexican blankets also came in brightly colored patterns but they could cost five times as much as those made with natural undyed yarns.

Still in the textile department, Fort Uncompahgre stocked a variety of silk and cotton bandanas and scarves. These were all purpose items long popular among the people of the Rio Grande Valley. Women used them as head and shoulder coverings, and men wore them tied around their heads underneath their hats which generally did not have sweat bands. Horsemen used the same arrangement during cold weather and pulled the scarves down over their ears. They often wore a second one around their necks year around. Scarves served as slings or bandages and were frequently used to filter debris out of drinking water. A related use, on hot summer days, was to dip the same versatile item in water and retie it around the head or neck to give relief from the punishing Southwest sun. Blankets were expensive and coffins were unavailable for wilderness burials, so a corpse often went to its final rest with nothing more than the owner's scarf covering his or her head and face. Its versatility caught on with the Indians as well as the Americans coming from the East. Most popular was a finished black silk scarf approximately thirty inches square.

The 1830 inventory at Fort Uncompahgre included a small quantity of finished clothing such as trousers, shirts, stockings and jackets. Eight robes were listed, two of which are identified as maroon church robes. The former most likely were items for fort personnel but with almost no record of religious services being held at the post, we can only surmise the use of the church robes.

The 1830 inventory lists substantial quantities of combs and mirrors. The former were generally made of animal horn although ivory and wood were available. Most popular was the "ridding" comb, which had two sets of teeth set back to back. The coarser side was used for grooming; the opposite side, with teeth set very close together, was slowly drawn through the hair to pick up head lice and break egg masses away from individual hair shafts. This was a problem of the time that respected no cultural boundaries.

Mirrors were usually three inches in diameter, came in folding leather or metal cases and were backed with a mixture of tin and mercury. They were especially popular among Ute warriors who customarily wore a certain amount of face paint year around. Face paints were made from naturally occurring mineral earths, ground very fine and mixed with rendered animal fat. Red was almost impossible to produce in this manner so the trading post carried vermillion, a powdered mixture consisting primarily of mercuric sulfide. Mixed with fat and worn on the face for indefinite periods of time, it is believed that some wearers might have suffered from degrees of mercury poisoning. Beads came from Europe and were either ceramic or glass. At Fort Uncompahgre, the majority were about the size of a common garden pea, or slightly smaller, and came in a variety of colors. Those made of glass were particularly prized. When Robidoux first came into the region, Indian customers were willing to trade one prime beaver pelt for as few as three or four dark blue translucent glass beads.

A variety of miscellaneous goods were available through the years that Robidoux's trading post was in operation. Brass thimbles were introduced and they traded well. However, rather than using them as intended, Ute women punched holes in the bottoms and sewed them close enough together on their dresses so that they would jingle as the wearer moved. Small embroidery scissors were also attached to dresses as decoration. In time, tin plates, coffee pots, and other items of cookware became popular. Judging from shipping manifests, it would appear that most Indian ladies were more pragmatic about their purchases than their male counterparts. Luxury items did not appear to play that big of a roll in the busy lives of women.

With the men, it was a different story. Warriors made extensive use of beads as well as large quantities of brass tacks. Driven into leather and clinched or used to decorate gun stocks and saddles, tacks were extremely popular for decorative purposes. Men also had a weakness for specialty knives, daggers and, in some cases, swords and surplus military uniforms. They often acquired ceremonial tomahawks which were hollowed out to double as tobacco pipes.

Leaf tobacco was shipped west in three ways. Leaves were securely bound with cordage into cylindrical packages weighing from one to three pounds. They were also twisted into a closed tear drop shape that weighed from two to eight ounces. The most popular method was to treat tobacco leaves with a mixture of molasses and licorice before pressing it together in a rectangular iron mold. The resulting plug was not only more compact and resistant to the perils of weather and moisture, but maintained its quality for longer periods of time. Plug tobacco had an additional advantage. The user could bite off a chunk, chew it, and then spit the mixture into a small leather pouch he wore around his neck. Once dried, the chewed leaves were available to be used a second time as pipe tobacco.

The Ute diet was also expanded by trade goods brought into the Uncompahgre Valley by the Robidoux pack mules. Tea became an instant favorite. Although loose tea was available, it was expensive and had to remain in sealed lead containers until shortly before being used. To counter this problem, Chinese tea merchants pressed masses of green tea leaves into approximately six by eight inch blocks less than one inch thick. Deep indentations were made so that each block could later be broken down into still smaller pieces about half the size of a deck of playing cards. An individual had only to shave off a small quantity of leaves with a knife and add hot water.

Coffee became a popular trade item and with it, Mexican sugar. With almost no natural sweeteners of their own, Ute coffee drinkers

The introduction of trade goods, such as scissors, beads, needles and linen thread, opened the door for Ute women to create clothing that was elegant yet functional.

Oil on canvas, copyright 1998, Dan Deuter

liked to add a liberal amount of raw brown, cane sugar imported from Mexico. This came in hard, cone shaped pieces about the size of an old fashioned ice cream cone. Chocolate, salt, pepper, allspice, dry biscuits, vinegar, flour, and rice were available but more as luxury items.

In addition, the trade room at Fort Uncompahgre stocked the infamous Taos Lightning. Joseph Robidoux, oldest brother and clan patriarch, took a dim view of the liquor trade but his influence apparently ended in Missouri.

Distillery documents from Taos are still in existence that implicate his brother Antoine. It is not known when Antoine entered the liquor trade, but the first distillery was built near Taos in 1825 and within a few years several more followed. Known collectively as Taos Lightning, the product was grain alcohol, crystal clear and devoid of taste. Too concentrated to drink straight, the distillery product was cut with water by one-third up to two-thirds. Color could be obtained by adding dissolved gunpowder and/or tobacco leaves. Taste was manipulated by a combination of molasses and sugar. In many cases, hot Mexican chili peppers were suspended into the mixture and allowed to remain until their own fiery flavor had been leeched out by the liquor.

It became common, particularly from the 1830s on, for western traders to engage in the liquor trade even though it was against both United States and Mexican laws to trade alcohol to the Indian tribes. The statutes were almost impossible to enforce, and profit margins were high enough to tempt even scrupulous men. Whiskey, available in Taos for seventy-five cents a pint, could be moved a hundred miles north or west, cut with water and resold for four dollars. Buffalo robe traders obtained high quality Indian tanned buffalo hides in eastern Colorado for thirty-five cents worth of Taos Lightning and then sold the robes in St. Louis for five dollars each. Although normally shrewd traders, Indians under the influence of liquor would often sell or trade their furs and hides at a fraction of the real value.

Taos Lightning was not the only illegal trade item found for sale at Fort Uncompahgre. Even higher profits were made by selling firearms. From the very beginning, Spanish laws prohibited the sale of guns to Indians. Settlers, almost always outnumbered by the native peoples of the southwest, had no desire to see potential adversaries better armed. Few Spaniards had firearms and even Spanish cavalry often relied, quite effectively, on long deadly lances and pure courage.

Far to the north, French and later British fur traders had no such qualms. Their business was to acquire furs. Indian trappers who carried firearms found they could venture—almost with impunity—into many regions occupied by people armed only with traditional weapons. As a result, fur traders set off an arms race. By the 1820s this struggle had reached the northern borders of Ute country. The Shoshone people, trading with the British operating out of the Washington and Oregon country, carried English muskets.

The Robidouxs were involved in the gun trade from the very beginning. Antoine's older brother Francois was detained by Mexican authorities in 1825 for trading firearms to the Utes. His trade goods were confiscated but later returned—along with a stern warning from Santa Fe officials. Very likely, to accommodate the weapons trade, Antoine developed a more direct route from Missouri to his trading posts in western Colorado. Contraband goods such as guns were diverted from the Santa Fe Trail before it turned south towards Raton Pass and were packed over Mosca Pass and across the San Luis Valley to connect with the mountain branch of the California Trail. The likelihood of being apprehended by Mexican authorities that far north of Taos was remote. Not only did the new route prove convenient for gun running but other goods were transported over it as well. Every dollar kept out of the hands of Mexican customs agents translated into that much more profit.

Mexican laws aside, Antoine's guns very likely prevented Shoshone raids into Ute territory. In addition, the trade was extremely profitable. In 1830, a smooth bore musket could be purchased in Missouri for $8 to $10, brought to Fort Uncompahgre and traded for as much as $700 worth of prime beaver pelts. The fort also stocked powder, lead and flints. Rather than sell these items in bulk, it was common to measure out charges of powder and an equal number of lead balls which were exchanged for a given quantity of animal pelts or skins. One record indicates that a tanned deer skin was worth from eight to ten charges of powder and ball.

Antoine's fort beside the cold, green waters of the Gunnison soon became a focal point for many of the Ute hunters, trappers and their wives. Indeed, it changed their lives. In a very short time, Indian trappers were able to move their families from the Stone Age to that of iron. The availability of cloth and blanketing material released Ute women from endless hours involved in preparing animal skins for clothing. Copper and iron kettles made food preparation easier, and muskets helped seal off and defend some of the best beaver country remaining in the West. ✦

About the same time Antoine Robidoux was building Fort Uncompahgre in western Colorado, other traders were setting up camp in the Uintah Basin. Antoine later established two additional forts in what was to become northeastern Utah.

Courtesy Dan Deuter

Chapter 4
Competition, Horses & Slaves

Antoine had become increasingly aware of the trapping and trading potential that lay to the northwest of Fort Uncompahgre in the Great Basin of what would someday become northeastern Utah. He had been into the region during his first trip west and had friends who had successfully trapped the area. He was also undoubtedly aware that the American Fur Company was operating in the Wyoming region, and that British trappers working for the Hudson Bay Company were trapping the Snake River country in southern Idaho. Within little more than a year of establishing Fort Uncompahgre, Antoine left it under the management of his brother Louis and led a party of trappers into Utah and then north into Idaho. Near the Snake River he met a brigade of Hudson Bay traders. The British seldom resorted to the head-to-head tactics of their American counterparts and the two groups enjoyed an amiable visit before Antoine and his men returned to the Uintah Basin of Utah to spend the winter. At that point in time the British seemed content to remain in the Idaho country but other competitors were already settled in the Uintah Basin.

About the same time Antoine Robidoux was building Fort Uncompahgre in western Colorado, two other traders set up camp in northeastern Utah between the confluence of the Whiterocks and Uintah Rivers. If the two men applied for and received a license from Mexican authorities, no record has been found attesting the fact. William Reed was an experienced fur trader and his partner, Denis Julien, had clerked some years earlier with various French traders on the Missouri River. The latter's latest employment had been with Antoine's brother Louis in the Santa Fe/Taos area. Reed's Trading Post, as the enterprise came to be known, was little more than a one-room, log structure next to the river. Inventory was limited, and from a logistical standpoint (including the problems of supply and distance from Santa Fe), it was impractical for two men to maintain such an operation. Although the venture did not prove out for its founders, it must have showed potential for Antoine. In September of 1831, he was granted a license by authorities in Santa Fe to expand his operation and to build a second fort. He bought Reed out in the spring of 1832. The former owner moved to California and his partner remained and went back to work for the Robidouxs.

Antoine abandoned Reed's cabin and built a new post further back from the river. Little is known about its physical appearance other than it consisted of several log buildings with dirt roofs and floors very similar to Fort Uncompahgre. Accounts differ as to whether it was surrounded by a stockade, but a substantial picket fence was probably erected as a corral for the animals. Unlike the post on the Gunnison, which existed primarily for the Ute Indian trade, Fort Uintah dealt with a wider circle of clients. From the beginning, a number of Anglo and Mexican trappers, some with their Indian families, lived near the post. Utah Utes found the location more convenient than making the journey to Fort Uncompahgre. With a gradual alliance developing between the Uintah Utes and their old enemies the Shoshones to the north, the latter also began making trading trips to Antoine's newest fort.

The post's proximity to the Snake River country made it convenient for Antoine and his employees to spend at least part of the trapping season in southern Idaho—on the doorstep of the Hudson Bay Company. For the moment, relations with the powerful British fur consortium remained amiable, perhaps because their employees were stretching their own limits in terms of distance from their home base in the northwest coastal region.

It was one of Antoine's New Mexico friends who next entered the Utah territory. In the fall of 1833, Kit Carson and several companions took pack horses loaded with trade goods out of Taos and followed the California Trail as far as the Uintah Basin and on to the confluence of the Green and White Rivers. They built three shelters—part dugout, part cabin—and spent the fall trapping and attempting to attract local Utes for trading. At one point they encountered Antoine and a party of twenty men trailing a thief who had stolen one of Antoine's favorite horses. Carson took up the chase alone, followed the stolen animal and

Horses and pack mules were used to carry supplies and trade goods in and hides and furs out of the trading posts established by Robidoux and his competitors.

Courtesy Dan Deuter

its rider for 130 miles, killed the man and brought the horse back. On good terms with Carson and his group, Antoine returned to Santa Fe to spend the winter of 1833-34. When spring arrived, Carson and his party, having been unsuccessful in trading with the Utes, sold their goods and the furs they had taken to Antoine's brother Louis and proceeded north into Wyoming—apparently content to leave the Uintah Basin trade to the Robidouxs. Horse stealing was apparently an ongoing problem, because sometime later an unknown party stopped near Fort Uncompahgre long enough to make off with more of Antoine's horses. Two unnamed black trappers regained possession of the animals and returned them. Antoine rewarded both men with company employment.

Throughout the 1820s, trappers had received from five to six dollars per pound for beaver furs with a large, prime pelt weighing up to a pound and a half after it had been scraped clean and dried. During this same period of time, eastern farmers were paying a little more than one dollar an acre for farm land. There were few ways a man could get rich quicker than to be successfully involved in some aspect of the beaver trade, but that was about to change. During the early 1830s, expanding world trade brought growing quantities of Chinese silk to Europe. Hat makers who had been using beaver felt for decades discovered that hats could be made from silk—hats that were stylish for both men and women, lighter in weight and cooler to wear in the summer. Markets responded positively and silk hats became the rage among Europe's upper and middle classes. Trappers in South America had also entered European markets with pelts from animals very similar to the beaver. Nutria, an aquatic rodent much smaller than its North American cousin, and with a rat-like tail, were found in jungle wetlands in prodigious numbers. Although not the same high quality as beaver, nutria fur was similar enough to make good felt. As a result, top hats that had previously cost as much as an average working man made in one month, were now within the economic reach of the laboring class. Even American hat makers began importing the cheaper South American fur to make hats. The combined effects of silk and nutria devastated the American beaver trade. Prices plummeted, but perhaps it was just as well. Nearly two centuries of trapping in North America had seriously reduced the beaver population. All this took place just as Antoine Robidoux was consolidating his hold on the western valleys of Colorado and the basins of eastern Utah. Optimistic like others in his trade, he believed the drop in beaver prices would be only temporary—meanwhile, there were other ways to survive.

The Robidouxs built a tannery in Santa Fe and began taking in furs and hides of every description. There was a constant demand for leather and furs in eastern American markets, and the brothers continued making use of Santa Fe freight wagons to carry these items back to St. Joseph. Antoine also began promoting Indian-tanned deer and mountain sheep skins. Unlike chemically tanned leather, buckskin was produced by mechanically working a cleaned and de-haired skin that had been softened with animal brains.

The damp hide was pulled and stretched until it became soft and dry. In the next step, it was treated with smoke, which prevented the fibers from pulling together and becoming stiff and hard. The entire process, from removing the hair to smoking, took roughly eight hours of labor per skin. Well-made buckskin was soft, warm, could stand repeated soakings and wore very well. Making the product required a great deal of skill and unless properly done, the finished fabric often had an uneven degree of softness. Nevertheless horsemen, army officers and those who could afford them, had worn buckskin trousers, gloves and jackets since prerevolutionary times. No tribe west of the Mississippi had a reputation that surpassed the Ute women for making quality buckskin. Antoine cashed in on that fact and was able to sell all that his Indian suppliers brought him.

Although no longer a big money maker, beaver pelts continued to play a roll in western trade and all through the 1830s the rich, glossy, round skins came into the trade rooms at Forts Uncompahgre and Uintah. Trappers and traders alike clung to hope that the prices would return to 1820 levels. Most did not understand the changes that had been brought into play by expanding world trade and the changing whims of European fashion. For decades, beaver pelts had been so stable in value that they had come to be referred to as "hairy bank notes"— and were often be used in that regard.

For Antoine's Indian customers who had shared in only a few years of the beaver prosperity, there seemed a dark side to the decline in pelt values. Although the prices for skins had decreased dramatically, the cost of trade goods remained the same. The Utes had no way to understand why a pelt, worth seven dollars in 1829 brought no more than a dollar or two in 1835. Although they continued to hunt, trap, and trade, suspicion grew that perhaps they were being cheated. To make matters worse, traders traditionally gave better trades to Anglo and Mexican customers than they did to the Indians. The Utes had no other choice, so they began taking advantage of other products the trader was willing to take in exchange for the items behind his counters.

Beaver of both sexes contain two prune-sized glands near their anal area from which they release fluid to mark territory. Trappers had long used the substance, known as castoreum, to bait the site where a trap was set. Strongly territorial, an unsuspecting beaver would investigate, hoping to find out more about the suspected intruder and would usually catch a foot in the waiting iron trap. Instinct immediately drove the animal out into deep water where the heavy trap, attached to a long chain, quickly pulled it under to drown.

By the 1830s, castoreum had gained favor in medical circles for treating hysteria, earache, abscesses, gout, headache, liver problems, epilepsy and even insanity. What physicians were not aware of was that the glands contained substantial quantities of salicin—very similar to the active ingredient contained in modern aspirin. Willow bark was a favorite food for beaver and salicin found in the bark became concentrated within the scent glands. During the skinning process the glands were removed, dried and shipped east to be processed into medicinal powders. As the substance gained wider use, demand drove up the price and gave western trappers an extra financial niche.

It did not matter if you were Indian, Mexican or American. Trapping beaver was a cold, dirty and often tedious way to make a living. Ed Maddox, trapper and historical interpreter at the reconstructed Fort Uncompahgre, demonstrates how to scrape down a dry beaver hide.

Courtesy *Delta County Independent*

Beyond bales of beaver pelts, animal hides and bags of castoreum, Fort Uncompahgre became known for two other items of commerce— Indian slaves and California horses. From the very beginning of the Spanish presence in the New World, it had been the custom to place native peoples into involuntary bondage. This practice continued for several reasons. First, a high percentage of the Spanish who came to the new world were members of the elite classes of Spain. As a result, there were never enough working class citizens in the new colonies, leaving a shortage of servants and agricultural workers. No Spaniard wanted to labor in the growing number of gold and silver mines. Nor was it to the advantage of high-born settlers to encourage immigration of working class Spaniards when slave labor was so readily available and free for the taking. The practice was also justified as a short cut towards civilizing the Indian people and converting them to the Christian faith.

When Spanish settlers reached the Rio Grande Valley of New Mexico in the early 1600s, they brought Indian slaves with them. Comanche, Apache and Ute raiders found the newcomers to be willing customers for children captured from weaker tribes. Captives were often given religious training and baptized into the Church where, by law, they were entitled to citizen rights. The New Mexican frontier was perpetually short of marriageable women and when an Indian slave girl reached the age of fourteen, her owner generally made the necessary provisions for her marriage. Almost always this was to a young man who was of mixed parentage himself, part European and part Indian.

Young male slaves, once they attained the age of eighteen to twenty, were commonly adopted into the households where they had been raised and were given the family name. In some instances, Ute families voluntarily left their children with a Spanish family to raise and educate. The famous Ute leader Ouray spent his boyhood years herding sheep for a Mexican family. There were some exceptions. Boys, purchased for work in the mines, seldom lived more than a few years before succumbing to disease, injury or overwork. Conditions were often little better for young women forced into marriages over which they had no control.

Finally, under pressure from the Catholic Church, which had long taken a dim view of the practice, Spain issued a decree in 1778 which forbid the taking of any more slaves. The edict was largely ignored, particularly in the northern colonies. A second ban against the practice was proclaimed in 1812 with the same futile results. Shortly after Mexico gained her independence from Spain, the new government passed a national law forbidding slavery of any form in all the lands controlled by the Mexican government. Again, the law had little effect on the northern colonies, particularly in and around Santa Fe. Slave laborers and wives were still very much in demand.

Powerful Indian tribes around the region, particularly the Utes, came to depend on the trade. They raided their weaker neighbors, capturing young boys and girls and exchanging them for trade goods or horses. Generally, they could deal directly with Mexican traders who ventured out and away from the settled regions and were therefore able to avoid Mexican authorities or army patrols that might intervene. The traders, when returning to Taos and Santa Fe, had little trouble eluding the thinly stretched arms of the law.

If caravans were intercepted, it was easy enough for traders to say they had rescued their little captives and were hoping for nothing more than to find the children suitable homes. Authorities, not knowing where the human contraband had come from, had little choice but to do exactly that—although the traders lost their expected profits. When slave traders were successful, which was most of the time, the families who bought the children had only to fabricate their own story of where the child had come from and take out adoption papers. There was almost nothing authorities could do from that point because it was difficult to physically separate slave children from those of local Indian/Spanish heritage.

American traders who entered the Santa Fe trade in the 1820s gave little thought to the practice, often bringing their own African slaves with them which they listed on passport papers as hired servants. Americans who remained in the capital purchased native children for their own households. A few, such as Antoine Robidoux, entered into the Indian slave trade as a side line to his other trading ventures.

Once Fort Uncompahgre was established, Ute raiders found it a convenient market for captives. Raids against the weaker Paiute bands further west were increased and raiding parties sometimes rode as far as the Pacific coastal states. In 1830, boys between the ages of eight and twelve were worth from $50 to $100 in trade goods. Girls were worth twice as much. When a mule caravan returned to Taos, Antoine usually sent the young captives along to be discreetly sold for Spanish silver. Since the practice was illegal, customs agents were never involved. The entire venture was tax free, carried little risk and almost no overhead.

A beaver skull, two pair of dried castor glands and a top hat—all resting on the rich fur of a Colorado beaver. In 1830, a top quality hat similar to this one could easily have cost the average working man an entire month's wages.

Ken Reyher photo

Perhaps the best description of the slave trade at Fort Uncompahgre can be found in an account written by Joseph Williams, a Methodist clergyman returning from Oregon in 1842. The Reverend spent several days at the post and upon leaving for New Mexico made a passing comment that the Robidoux traders carried with them several slaves including adult females and children of both sexes. The party was held up when two of the women escaped not far from the fort. After two days of futile searching, the Robidoux party sent back for one Indian captive who had been left at the fort, then continued on towards Santa Fe. Williams seemed more irritated by the delay than he did by the fact the party was dealing in human flesh.

Without horses, it would have been impossible to open the West to trade and commerce. Introduced to these animals by the Spanish as early as the 1600s, a majority of western Indian tribes quickly became mobile and began to range far beyond their traditional territories. Although some tribes bred and raised their own mounts, most depended on capturing wild horses or trading and raiding for them in the settlements. In addition, settlers in the Rio Grande Valley of New Mexico also needed horses beyond their capacity to breed and raise them. American trappers and traders relied on western animals and the Missouri frontier was a ready market for any surplus mules that could be trailed east.

One place where an excess of horses and mules existed was the pastures of California. For over 200 years, first Spanish and then Mexican settlers had allowed their herds to multiply, and by the early 1800s, California contained extensive numbers of both horses and mules. Although the ranchers claimed ownership, many herds were allowed to roam free without supervision. That fact was not lost on Mexican horse raiders from Santa Fe or a growing number of American mountain men. It proved simple enough to ride into a California valley, round up a sizable herd and point it east over the California Trail towards New Mexico. The fact that they could be traded or sold at Fort Uintah or Fort Uncompahgre, shortened the trip as much as 400 miles. Like slaves, horses and mules were high dollar items, and a sizable herd might easily net more profit than a man could hope to accumulate in his entire life time. ✦

Antoine's brother Louis, seen here, was aware that conditions were deteriorating in New Mexico during the late 1830s. He sold his holdings and moved his family to California where he became a successful rancher. Mount Robidoux, near Riverside, California bears his name today.

Courtesy Museum of New Mexico

Chapter 5
A Time of Change

While Antoine was involved in the California horse trade, unprecedented changes were taking place east of the Rocky Mountains. From the plains region, buffalo robes were being shipped to St. Louis by the hundreds of thousands. The eastern states were entering the Industrial Revolution and the south was beginning to turn its future towards cotton. In the southwest and other regions west of the Rocky Mountains, change was also evident but it was not something welcomed by those it affected. For the Mexican people, free ranging Indians and men like Antoine Robidoux, a way of life was nearing its end.

Once the only trading establishments in the region, Antoine's forts were now up against small groups of itinerant and unlicensed traders. Men who could no longer make a living in trapped out areas to the east and north, began filtering into Antoine's domain with a few packs of goods hoping to turn a profit before moving on. Occasionally, their attempts proved more long term.

Brown's Hole, located in extreme northwestern Colorado, had long been a popular wintering ground for mountain men and trappers. In 1836, Thomas Biggs and two companions, all former employees of fur companies that had operated on the Platte River between present day Denver and Greeley, built a trading post near Vermillion Creek. They named it Fort Davy Crockett, in honor of the popular frontiersman who had recently lost his life in the Texas Alamo. Consisting of no more than a collection of huts—it lacked even a stockade—the new owners soon learned that they were in the wrong place at the wrong time.

Isolation made the post hard to supply and even basic items were often unavailable. Squatting on Mexican territory without proper authorization, it is likely the fort received its supplies directly overland from St. Louis. Fort Davy Crockett was, at times, reduced to buying supplies from Robidoux men. Antoine did not take Fort Crockett to be a serious threat to his own operation. Most likely, its owners paid Antoine retail prices because records show Fort Crockett's selling prices were higher than those charged at Fort Uncompahgre. The post at Brown's Hole also found itself competing with traders coming out of southern Wyoming who were willing to sell for less. One went so far as to set up a teepee within sight of the post on Vermillion Creek and offered knives, hatchets, powder, lead, fishhooks and whiskey. Not particularly interested in furs, the teepee trader preferred cash or horses. Within little more than a year, Fort Davy Crockett came to be known as Fort Misery. At one point its occupants, out of food and unsuccessful in hunting, were forced to purchase and eat several dogs from local Indians. The incident probably amused the Utes sellers who viewed dog meat as starvation food, nevertheless they demanded and received fifteen dollars in Mexican silver for each animal.

British traders who had long made southern Idaho a southeastern boundary line for their area of operations, began to compete for trade in the regions of Utah long held secure by Antoine. Known for their lower-than-average prices on trade goods and cordial relations with most Indian tribes, it is likely the Hudson Bay people were attempting to increase profits by increasing volume. Apparently Antoine viewed this attempt as a threat far more serious than either that of Fort Crockett or of the itinerant traders wanting horses and silver. He decided to build a third trading post, which was called Fort Robidoux. It is doubtful that it was anything more than a temporary trading site used for a short time, then abandoned. Few facts about the venture have survived other than that Antoine himself left an inscription on a large sandstone rock not far from the Colorado/Utah border northwest of Grand Junction, Colorado. The inscription, in French, still exists today and reads: "Antoine Robidoux passed here 13 November 1837 to establish a trading post at the Green and White River."

In 1838, Hudson Bay officials, possibly in retaliation, attempted to build a fort at the confluence of the Green and Duchesne Rivers— right in Antoine's backyard and clearly on Mexican soil. Acting in his own interest and as a legitimate representative of the Mexican government, Antoine brought his own men to the site and attempted to confiscate the opposition's horse herd. Unable to put their animals out to graze for fear of losing them, the Hudson Bay men soon abandoned their venture and returned to Idaho, leaving their adversary firmly in control of the Uintah Basin. Fort Robidoux was abandoned about the same time. The battle might have continued, but the price for beaver pelts remained so low that investors in the big companies like Hudson Bay were calling for consolidation rather than expansion.

A final effort to penetrate the western mountain trade was made in 1839 when employees from Bent's Fort, located along the Arkansas River in southeastern Colorado, crossed over into the Uintah Basin. The local Utes demanded tribute from the trade party for entering Ute land. The traders refused and after a brief skirmish with the warriors, the Bent men turned their pack train around and returned to more familiar territory in the plains country east of the mountains.

Although his trading empire still appeared to be solid, cracks were developing along Antoine's supply line from Saint Joseph to Santa Fe. Like the Utes, Indians controlling the plains of Kansas and Colorado had learned to demand tribute and crossing fees from the caravans of wagons coming west. With as many as thirty different tribal entities associated with the trail, such expenses added up, but they could be regained by price increases in Santa Fe. Freighters also raised rates received for hauling hides, furs and other items on the return trip. Even the Mexican government reached deeper into the pockets of traders. Import tariffs and taxes which totaled three percent in 1824 reached twenty percent by 1840. Not all of the increase can be blamed on the tax officials. American freighters and traders had developed a variety of ways to cheat. Antoine himself chose to bring both illegal and high-cost items directly over the mountains far north of Santa Fe to avoid paying customs.

Trappers—Indian, Mexican and Anglo alike—were still bringing in pelts and skins of every kind by the late 1800's, although low prices had already encouraged many to quit. Indian traders complained about unemployed and hard drinking Americans who had taken up residence in or near the forts. It had also become increasingly popular for former mountain men to steal horses for the markets in Santa Fe. The Utes themselves had become targets of some of these thieves.

Servants and wives remained in strong demand as New Mexico continued its climb to material affluence. The practice of taking Indian children continued, and the ten or twelve-year-old child who might have brought one or two hundred dollars in trade goods in 1830, had increased in value to twice that amount. Raids, particularly against the smaller and weaker bands of Indians living in Utah and Nevada, increased, and raiders began taking young adult women as well.

A decade of trading and raiding had brought material affluence to the Utes, the Shoshone and others. Knives and hatchets, items to be treasured a few years earlier, were now common. Blankets, cloth and other industrial items were rapidly replacing buckskin. Firearms, once nearly unattainable at $700 each were now plentiful and selling for the price of a good horse. The fiery alcohol known as Taos Lightning was making inroads into the lives and cultures of the native peoples. The Indian way of life, stable for centuries, was entering a period of turmoil and change.

Meanwhile, Antoine found himself facing yet another problem. A new trail was beginning to open across the heart of the continent towards Oregon and California. Trade wagons had crossed South Pass into western Wyoming as early as 1830, but it was not until 1841 that the first immigrants made it all the way to the coast. Almost overnight,

Robidoux believed that the conduit to the coast would follow the Santa Fe and the California Trails and built three forts along this route. By 1840, the opening of the Oregon Trail further to the north continued to undermine Antoine's already declining empire.

Courtesy Dan Deuter

the Oregon Trail became the primary conduit across the West. While most of its history has been written by and about the people who crossed it, the trail also became one of the most important freighting roads in America. Traders were especially quick to exploit the new route. Stopping places like Fort Bridger in southwestern Wyoming and Fort Hall in southern Idaho quickly became new trading hubs for the mountain west. Freight rates were lower than on the Santa Fe Trail and by 1840, increasing competition among eastern manufacturers allowed for decreasing prices of goods as well. Customers, both Indian and non-Indian alike found trade along the new trail very much to their liking. With Fort Uintah more than 100 miles south of the trail and committed to Santa

Fe contracts, Antoine began to lose long-time customers to the new competition. Making matters worse, most western Indians, understanding neither the logistics of the new trail or the forces unleased by the Industrial Revolution in the east, began to murmur that perhaps the Robidoux trading posts had been cheating them over the years with high prices.

Meanwhile, Antoine began focusing his attention more on the growing demand for horses and mules and less on events at the trading counter. By 1840, almost any Indian pony was worth fifty dollars. Mexican horses out of California brought one hundred dollars each, and well bred horses from the east sold for as much as $500. An increasing number of animals were rustled from California ranches. Mustangs running in the basins west of the mountains were available to those willing to chase them down. Several Indian tribes, including the Utes, were engaged in breeding programs that resulted in animals rivaling many of the blooded horses coming from the eastern states. Lack of fences and minimal supervision often allowed western stock to escape and wander hundreds of miles until reclaimed by someone else. The days of hanging horse thieves was still a generation in the future. However, there were limits.

In 1840, one of the owners of Fort Crockett and several followers—burning from the loss of nearly one hundred head of horses taken by either a far ranging Cheyenne or Sioux war party—decided to do a little raiding of their own. Traveling into southwestern Wyoming, they stole fourteen animals near Fort Hall. A few days later, after spending the night with a band of peaceful Shoshone, they took thirty animals from their hosts' herd before continuing south. Before they reached Fort Crockett the group was intercepted by friends from the fort who voiced their wrath after learning where the horses had originated. There was more. Three of the West's most famous mountain men, Kit Carson, Joe Meek and Joseph Walker (along with thirty followers), were approaching from the north. The horse thieves fled for their lives, taking only the animals they were riding. The Carson party returned the stolen horses to their owners, but the event so badly tainted the already shaky reputation of Fort Crockett that it went out of business a few weeks later.

Records exist for only one of Antoine's horse trading ventures. In December of 1841, he left St. Louis with a herd of more than 400 animals and pointed them southwest down the Santa Fe Trail. Ahead ran a second herd owned by his long-time friend and supplier, Don Manuel Alvarez. In January, on Cottonwood Creek near Council Grove, Kansas, a killer blizzard struck both parties. Two men from the Alvarez party froze to death as did most of the herd. Antoine's stock was also lost. His entire $40,000 investment lay dead and frozen across the Kansas prairie or had drifted so far as to be irretrievable. With several men suffering from frostbite, messengers were dispatched to Saint Joseph and a relief expedition rescued both parties and returned them to Missouri. That spring, Antoine continued on to Santa Fe and his trading posts.

Little is known about activities at either Fort Uncompahgre or Fort Uintah from that point other than brief accounts by three very different visitors. In 1842, Reverend Joseph Williams, returned from a tour of the Oregon country and stopped at Fort Uintah where he hoped to accompany a Robidoux pack train on to Santa Fe. Williams had met Antoine a year earlier when the preacher was on his way to the coast and for unknown reasons, had developed an immediate dislike for the trader. The minister's eighteen-day stay at the fort left one of the few recorded eyewitness accounts. None of it was flattering. In his book, *Narrative Of A Tour From The State Of Indiana To The Oregon Territory In the years 1841-2,* he wrote:

"This morning July 9, 1842, we had some frost.... This delay was very disagreeable to me, on account of the wickedness of the people, and the drunkenness and swearing, and the debauchery of the men among the Indian women. This place is equal to any I ever saw for wickedness and idleness. The French and Spaniards are all Roman Catholic: but are as wicked men, I think as ever lived. No one who has not, like me, witnessed it, can have no idea of their wickedness. Some of these people at the Fort are fat and dirty, and idle and greasy."

That they were dirty, idle and greasy can be accepted as an apt description for the average frontier trapper in the middle of July—and food was apparently abundant at Fort Uintah that year.

When the reverend reached Fort Uncompahgre, he encountered another delay. He was no more impressed there than at Fort Uintah. He did, however, preach at least one sermon, which he said was well attended, an interesting fact considering that the Protestant minister's impromptu congregation was, as he himself stated, mostly Roman Catholic. More than likely, his was the only formal religious service

In less than a decade Antoine's trade goods had lifted the Ute people from an age of stone and animal skins to one of iron and calico cloth.

Courtesy Fort Uncompahgre

ever held at the post. Five days out of Fort Uncompahgre and some-where in the Gunnison Valley, Williams recorded that, "...we came to Rubedeau's [sic] wagon, which he had left here the year before. He hitched his oxen to it, and took it along." The caravan continued and picked up an unexpected rumor about possible Ute Indian hostilities in the San Luis Valley but the journey was completed and they reached Taos without further incident.

The next mention of Fort Uncompahgre came later that same year when Marcus Whitman, a missionary doctor in the Oregon country, received word to close down two mission settlements and send several of his fellow missionaries home. He chose instead to risk a 3,000 mile journey across the continent in the dead of winter to argue the order with his superiors. First snows were already on the ground in 1842 when Whitman and a companion, Asa Lovejoy, arrived at Fort Uncompahgre, destitute and starving. They had eaten their pack animals as well as their pet dog and were hoping to make their way on to Taos. Provided with necessary supplies and a guide, the travelers took the shorter but more brutal mountain route and arrived in Taos in mid-December. The two men continued their journey east, and Whitman won his point: the missions remained open. He returned west the following summer. If the doctor shared William's sentiments about Fort Uncompahgre, he did not record them.

The third written account regarding Antoine's trading posts came when John Freemont visited Fort Uintah in June of 1844. Brought to the post by his guide, Kit Carson, the explorer purchased supplies and hired Denis Julien as an additional member for his expedition to California. Julien had been associated with Fort Uinah since its founding twelve years earlier. The reason he left is open to speculation, but most likely he hoped that a better future lay elsewhere. Like Reverend Williams, Freemont was not impressed with the fort, writing little more than it consisted of a "...motley garrison...of Canadians, Spanish *engages* and hunters with their Indian women." Although he did not know it at the time, Freemont and his men were the last visitors of record. Time had run out for Antoine's forts. ✦

Courtesy Dan Deuter

Chapter 6
A Time for War

By 1840, Antoine was aware that long-standing peaceful relations between the Utes and Santa Fe were deteriorating. Many of the younger warriors within the Ute bands had grown resentful towards Mexicans. The Utes had long attempted to make it clear that permanent settlers were not welcome on tribal lands, but Mexican farmers and ranchers had been slowly moving north until they were inside the boundaries of the San Luis Valley, long a favorite summer camping and hunting ground for some of the southern Utes. Although the situation was tolerated for the moment, the Indians argued among themselves about a solution. More problems came as traffic increased on the California Trail. Utes began demanding payment to cross through. Mexican packers balked and viewed the attempts to collect as little more than begging.

The cheaper prices with which goods were being acquired from the new trading posts along the Oregon Trail added to Ute unrest as did the continuing stagnation of fur prices. To make matters worse, the beaver were now almost gone—trapped out. Recognizing that fact, American mountain men held their last rendezvous the summer of 1840. Ute trappers had been forming a simmering suspicion that they had long been cheated by Santa Fe and Taos. In one respect the charge was true, because Mexican and American mountain men had always received more for pelts than their Indian counterparts. Unrest increased further when unscrupulous traders began bringing in increasing quantities of

Taos Lightning, the result of which was beginning to affect Ute society. Even the trading posts had become places for drunken and idle trappers to harass Ute women coming to trade. Tempers frayed still further when increasing numbers of Ute horses began disappearing—victims of thieves. Fuel for a fire had been laid, and it only needed a spark.

During the summer of 1843, Navajo warriors raided several ranches west of Santa Fe. Cries for vengeance were answered by an expedition of volunteers out of the territorial capital who rode out in search of the raiders. Frustrated in their attempts to locate the Navajo, the Mexican militia fell upon a peaceful camp of Utes. They killed ten people, captured three more and took possession of the camp's livestock. As word of the atrocity spread north through the Ute camps, young warriors demanded revenge, but their cries were initially ignored. Instead, it was decided to send a delegation to Santa Fe and talk directly with the Mexican governor.

On September 7, 1844, six Ute chiefs and more than 100 armed warriors entered Santa Fe. People cleared the streets as the entourage rode to the town square and halted before the Palace of Governors. The six leaders went inside where they met with the governor and his deputies. Minutes into the meeting a fight broke out, and one of the Ute chiefs was killed. The remaining five retreated into the street where they and their warriors engaged in a pitched battle with Mexican soldiers and Santa Fe citizens. The Utes fought their way out of the city, and losing seven more of their number before gaining the safety of open country. There would be no more talking. The time for killing had come.

Riding northwest along the California Trail, the enraged Utes made the unsuspecting Mexican village of Abiquiu their first target. Ten of the town's inhabitants lost their lives. Momentarily sated, the warriors broke away from the trail and turned northeast towards the hated ranches and farms located on Ute land in the San Luis Valley. Their goal was to burn out and kill every settler they found. Before they were finished, more than 100 Mexican men, women and children, lay dead. Still wanting revenge, warriors rode up Cochetopa Pass, down into the Gunnison Valley and west towards Antoine Robidoux's trading posts which were staffed almost entirely by Mexican employees.

Only one known eyewitness account survives regarding the attack on Fort Uncompahgre, and it leaves almost as many questions as it does answers. In late September, Jose Francisco Trujillo and Calario Cortez were somewhere downstream from the fort checking traps. They were far enough away that they did not hear the attack on the fort. Cortez was barefoot and in the water. His rifle and other gear lay yards away up on the bank near Trujillo. Suddenly, shots rang out and Trujillo fell

mortally wounded. More bullets splashed into the water around Cortez as he made his way to the stream's edge, up the bank and into the underbrush. Leaving his dead companion and all his own gear behind, Cortez began a race for his life.

He reached the fort only to find his fellow employees slaughtered, their women gone and the trade goods taken. Knowing his pursuers were a short distance behind, the Mexican mountain man, still barefoot and without a coat, headed south and kept out of

Gunpowder was sold in wooden kegs tightly sealed and wrapped with hoops of split willow.
Courtesy *Delta County Independent*

sight as he made his way through the undergrowth along the Uncompahgre River. Using skills with which he had become adept, Cortez left very little trail for the warriors to follow and when nightfall came, left even less. After reaching the present location of Montrose, he turned east up Cedar Creek towards Cerro Summit. Hiding during the day and traveling only at night, the trapper worked his way east into the Gunnison Valley, avoiding the trail and following the rocks, making it nearly impossible for his pursuers to follow. It is possible, once he was certain the Utes had given up, that he made use of a small cabin Antoine had built some years previously at the top of Cochetopa Pass.

Finally, after fourteen days, ragged and still barefoot, he walked into Taos—exhausted and hungry but alive. A modest man, Cortez gave almost no details of his successful escape, but facts speak for themselves. With nothing more than wit and courage, he had foiled the efforts of some of the best trackers in the world and survived their pursuit as well as the first mountain snows of October.

What Calario Cortez was not aware of was that the Ute raiders had captured an unnamed American who had been at the fort. They later released him with instructions to find Antoine Robidoux and tell him the furs, hides, and buildings had been left intact. Their quarrel was only with Mexico and not the Americans or French. No record exists as to Antoine receiving that message, but it is likely the American from Fort Uncompahgre headed straight for Fort Uintah and warned its inhabitants, because seven of its employees equipped themselves from that post's store room, mounted company mules and made their escape east through the mountains—all this just days after the fall of Fort Uncompahgre. It is not known if any of Antoine's men remained behind, and no eyewitness account ever surfaced regarding Fort Uintah's actual destruction. However, Antoine later left a letter describing property the seven men had taken with them in their escape to Pueblo and wrote that he still hoped to collect for its value. Either another party gave him that information or he returned to the post and discovered what was missing.

Another question for which there is no answer is why the Utes allowed Fort Uintah to be warned at all, because Mexican employees worked there as well. Mounted and well-armed, the warriors would have had little trouble surprising the post and preventing any escape. One possibility is that they spent too much time attempting to track down Cortez. Two months had passed since the fight in Santa Fe and the desire for revenge might have cooled. Another unanswered question remains. What was the motive of the Utes for leaving Fort Uncompahgre and its storeroom of furs and skins intact? Did they really want the trader to return with more trade goods and continue as if nothing had happened or were they baiting a trap to lure Antoine back so that he too could be killed? Some historians think that might have been the case, but Ute leaders had often spoken highly of the man who successfully traded in their midst for almost twenty years.

Forty years after the raids, white historians visited with aging warriors who would have known the answers, but little was provided in the way of new information. Forced to live on desert reservations—their children virtual hostages in distant, white boarding schools—the Utes might have feared white retribution if they told the whole story.

One known fact is that the governor in Santa Fe, a new and overly ambitious political appointee with no love for Americans, was quick to

Gunpowder was usually stored in an underground bunker designed so that if it blew up, the blast would be directed upward and away from surrounding structures. The powder magazine seen here is outside the trade room of the reconstructed Fort Uncompahgre.

Ken Reyher photo

place part of the blame for the Ute uprising directly on Antoine. He ordered an immediate investigation regarding the trader's sale of firearms to the Utes. Aware of the actions against her husband, Carmel closed their Santa Fe home and returned to Saint Joseph with her daughter. Antoine, who possibly spent several months in the Wyoming area, also returned east according to a story in the September 17, 1845, *Missouri Democrat*. The article briefly relayed the attack on Fort Uncompahgre and reported that three Mexican employees had been killed but that one American had been spared and used as a messenger to relay to Antoine that his pelts, hides and buildings were safe. An editorial comment ended the account by affirming that despite the Utes' desire for retribution against the Mexican people, they were "generally friendly to Americans." It isn't known who gave this information to the paper, but it would not appear that it came from Antoine. In addition, the number of employees killed was certainly more than three—Cortez indicated seeing six or seven bodies and he did not search the buildings. According to various accounts, the fort was allowed to remain standing two years after the attack before being destroyed by local Utes. Fort Uintah's fate is more uncertain, but at some point it was destroyed, and Antoine never returned to the mountains and valleys he had once controlled.

Within months of his return to Saint Joseph, the former trader found himself caught up in the war with Mexico. Despite having opened her borders to American traders in the early 1820s, the road between the two nations had never been smooth. Tariffs had risen steadily, traders sometimes had their goods confiscated for little or no reason, and they were often given second class treatment regarding legal matters they encountered while on Mexican soil.

There were other problems as well. Mexico and Texas had never agreed on a common border and perhaps most importantly, beginning in 1842, England had become involved in California. A British consul sent to the colony openly advocated its annexation to Great Britain. Mexico enticed that situation by offering the region to England in early

1846 as security for a loan. Americans, particularly western Americans, clamored for intervention by the federal government. President James Polk sent John Slidell to Mexico City with a harshly worded proposal demanding that Mexico assume responsibility for American financial claims in the northern provinces and that she sell both New Mexico and California to the United States for $25,000,000. Mexican sentiment was outraged to the point that Slidell was not even received by government officials. The die was cast and rebuffed Americans with western interests called for war. They got their wish through an alleged border altercation between Texas and Mexico. A divided Congress declared war on May 12, 1846. Several congressional leaders stood in opposition, including Abraham Lincoln, who achieved national recognition by demanding that President Polk provide proof of the so called "Texas Border Incident."

War drums were already beating. The army called for 50,000 volunteers to march against Mexico, although the Northeast and Southeast largely ignored the request. The westerners themselves filled the ranks and they did so willingly. One army invaded Texas, a second sailed south towards the Mexican capital and by early summer, a third force of 1,700 men marched west down the Santa Fe Trail towards New Mexico. Lead by Colonel Stephen Kearny, this western army included in its ranks the former trading kingpin of western Colorado, Antoine Robidoux. Listed on the rolls as guide and interpreter, the former trader played in important roll in negotiations a few weeks later in Santa Fe as Mexican officials in that provincial capital peacefully signed over the Rio Grande Valley to the Americans. Antoine might have enjoyed a moment of satisfaction as he faced some of the heavy handed bureaucrats who, only a year earlier, had attempted to blame him for the Ute uprising.

Following the conclusion of the New Mexico campaign, Kearny sent the majority of his troops south to join other American forces already in the interior. Then, with 300 hand-picked, mounted volunteers, he began a race to the west coast. One of his two guides was

The ultimate prize for a Ute warrior was a simple, rugged smooth bore flintlock gun like the one leaning against the stump. Originally made in England and later in America, this model proved so popular and reliable that the design did not change in almost 100 years. A small swivel cannon is secured to the stump.

Ken Reyher photo

Antoine Robidoux who might have made the trip a few years earlier when his brother Louis sold his Santa Fe business interests and moved his wife and children to a ranch near present day Riverside, California where the family resettled.

Partway to the coast, Kearny's command met Kit Carson and a small detachment racing east with papers from Commodore Stockton and explorer John Freemont proclaiming that California was in American hands. This was the first time Carson had seen his friend Antoine since he had led Freemont's expedition into Fort Uintah almost three years earlier. The ambitious Kearny—afraid he would miss out entirely on California's conquest—sent 200 of his men back to Santa Fe along with the dispatches. He ordered Carson, who knew where to connect with the Americans near San Diego, to join the remaining troops and return to the coast. The shorter but more punishing route through Arizona resulted in extreme hardship for both horses and soldiers, but Kearny insisted in pressing on at top speed.

On a rainy morning in December 1846, Kearny's worn-out men were within thirty miles of San Diego. Suddenly, out of the mists appeared a force of Mexican volunteers led by rancher Don Andres Pico. Only a few of his 133 men had muskets and rifles. The majority carried long cavalry lances, but behind them were their homes and families and though the coastal regions were now in American hands, they were determined to stop this latest threat from the interior.

Believing the threat minimal, Kearny divided his troops and charged Pico's ranchers. It was a fatal error. Many of the American's rain soaked weapons refused to fire and within minutes fierce hand-to-hand combat had left twenty of Kearny's men dead and nineteen more wounded. Antoine suffered a deep lance thrust into his lower back. Kit Carson had been thrown from his horse in the first moments of battle which probably saved him from injury or death. Kearny was seriously wounded. The only thing that saved his command was a hail of grape shot fired from a small howitzer stationed behind the line. In the face of cannon fire, the *Californios* retreated with several wounds but no deaths.

Pico's citizen-soldiers kept the Americans surrounded, picking away with their handful of firearms and being careful to avoid the howitzer. During the first night after the battle, Antoine, thought to be mortally wounded, was left to lay on the cold ground. It might have been that this act helped stop the bleeding. At first light the fifty-two year old former trapper and trader told those around him that he smelled fresh coffee. Believing the delirium of death had come—since the command had exhausted its supply of coffee weeks earlier—an officer knelt next to the wounded man to provide what comfort he could. Minutes later Antoine's personal servant arrived, carrying a hot cup of coffee and a dirt encrusted piece of hard, brown bread he had carried half way across Arizona beneath his shirt. Antoine insisted on sharing his breakfast with the officer—dirt and all.

Despite repeated efforts, the Americans found themselves unable break the grip of the opposing force. Finally, Carson made his way through the siege line and got word to San Diego where a relief column of some 200 American sailors marched out and rescued Kearny's men. Despite being the worst military disaster since the War of 1812, the belligerent colonel claimed the Battle of San Pasqual as an American victory on grounds that he had not given up the battlefield.

Antoine, still in serious condition from his wound and in great pain, was placed on a ship leaving San Diego. Having never been to sea, he began his recovery on the rolling, pitching deck. After a stop in Peru, the vessel continued around Cape Horn and sailed north to its next port of call in Jamaica. By the time it docked in New Orleans, the injury was sufficiently healed and Antoine was able to complete his journey to Saint Joseph with no assistance.

Changing circumstance had swept away the world of a man who once ruled a western empire. Financially ruined and never completely recovering from his wound, Antoine attempted a new beginning. In 1849, he contracted to guide an immigrant train of 137 wagons to California. Following a successful trip out and back, he spent the next few years involved with brothers and nephews trading along the Oregon

Trail. New trading posts were built along the route to provide goods and services for thousands of immigrants who moved west each summer. Once again the family found itself competing against an old nemesis, the American Fur Company. One company official wrote to his superiors complaining that one of the Robidouxs made a habit of stopping immigrant trains on the trail and would warn them that the American Fur traders at Fort Laramie were "all damned rascals and cheats." Family members made good profits by picking up abandoned property left along the trail and reselling it to other immigrants who came along later. The Robidouxs also engaged in the buffalo hide trade—again competing against American Fur employees. One Santa Fe Trail diary reported seeing six Robidoux wagons loaded with 3,000 buffalo hides. Another account mentioned eighteen wagon loads of hides tended by Robidoux employees—rough, greasy looking men who reminded the writer more of pirates than hide hunters.

For Antoine, the trading days were nearly over. Continued complications from the California wound began to impede his ability to walk or ride. To complicate matters, his vision deteriorated due to an hereditary eye condition that had long plagued the family. Finally, Antoine applied for and was granted, a small government pension for his Mexican War military service and then settled in Saint Joseph. The small fur trading village founded by his older brother little more than twenty years earlier had become a major gateway to the Pacific through which hundreds of thousands of western immigrants passed on their way west. Unable to walk and robbed of his sight, Antoine passed his final years, dependent on help from his wife and others. He died August 29, 1860 at the age of sixty five. ✦

Antoine Robidoux in his later years. Antoine never completely recovered from the lance wound he received during the Mexican War. Seen here near the end of his life, the man who once controlled a western trading empire spent his final days blind and unable to walk.

Courtesy Saint Joseph Historical Society

Chapter 7
Looking Back

Historians credit Antoine Robidoux with being the only trader in American history to have two of his posts destroyed by hostile action. Generally, commercial forts were peaceful places and the Utes had always been peaceful people—unless they felt their backs were against the wall. It would appear such had been the case in this instance. What had begun so promisingly in the middle 1820s crashed into ruin two decades later. New technology and the age of iron and steel had brought the Utes out of the Stone Age and into a time of technical advancement and change. However, the key to new ways and easier lives rode in the ninety pound packs of beaver pelts lashed to the sides of Antoine's pack mules. When prices crashed in the early 1830s, few people really understood exactly why—particularly the Utes. Time had also revealed more clearly the two-tiered pricing system that discriminated against Indian trappers as compared to Mexicans and Americans. Nor did the Indians understand how increasing industrial expansion in the east and the simultaneous opening of the Oregon Trail could lower prices that had remained constant for a generation. Their conclusion was that they had been cheated by the Santa Fe traders. This wasn't the end of the problems.

More and more outsiders had moved into Ute country following the California Trail and the Trappers Trail out of Idaho. Local sovereignty came under increasing pressure as the loosely bonded seven Ute bands found themselves less able to maintain traditional control over the vast territory they had roamed for hundreds of years. While willing to overlook, to a point, European and American incursions into their lands, young warriors began to draw the line with Mexican settlements in the San Luis Valley. Older men saw the effects whiskey traders were having. Horse thieves, no longer content with California herds, were stealing increasing numbers of Ute horses. It was the same with captives and slaves—the Utes themselves were beginning to fall victim as growing demands in New Mexico increased prices for marriageable women to $500 each.

Contrary to romantic notions of today, most early trappers and traders—the Americans, British, French, the Russians who came to California and the Spanish—entered the western and southwestern regions primarily in hopes of acquiring wealth. They made their own rules and did not hesitate to change them to fit the occasion. They were quick to embrace almost any situation or process which might increase profits. Caught up in these same dreams for wealth were the native peoples: one foot in a life they had known for generations, the other, balanced precariously in a world they could neither control nor fully comprehend.

Americans also carried the seeds of destruction for the Ute culture. It was trappers who made the first discoveries of placer gold in Ute territory. Within little more than a decade of the destruction of Antoine's forts, the miners came, and with them, towns, cattlemen, farmers and railroads. A way of life ended. But what of the man who had first controlled the non-Ute presence in western Colorado and the basins of Utah?

Antoine Robidoux was somewhat of a paradox. Six-foot tall and handsome, he could easily mingle with the highest placed men and women in either French or Mexican society. He was equally at home in greasy buckskins leading a trapping party or indulging in a marathon gambling game of *Hand* with a party of Ute hunters. Players would hold a small piece of carved bone or a painted plum seed, and then sing, dance and pass (or pretend to pass) the object from one clinched fist to the other. Finally, the other player would be asked to guess which hand the bone or plum pit was hidden in. Stakes could go high enough to include a favorite horse or a player's wife. Antoine enjoyed taking risks and often lived life itself as one continuing game of *Hand*.

If chance taking was a fault then it can also be said that loyalty was a virtue. Antoine was intensley loyal to those close to him. Despite long absences, his marriage to Carmel remained intact until his death, unlike that of many Americans who entered the Santa Fe Trade and married local women only to abandon them when convenient. Kit Carson, Joseph Walker, and other famous trappers of the day often went miles out of their way to visit his trading posts and do business with him. He remained steadfast to his Santa Fe business associates to the very end.

Antoine had his detractors as well. Mountain man Joe Meek accused him of being cruel, heartless and addicted to gambling. Meek, an accomplished story teller and no saint himself, gave the account in a series of interviews conducted thirty years after the fact. Antoine's willingness to take on the powerful Hudson Bay Company also made enemies. He led his men into country controlled by the British to trap and trade, but made every effort to keep Hudson Bay out of Mexican territory—something he had every right and even an obligation to do. Like most traders of his day, it is doubtful if many questions were asked regarding the origins of the horses for which he traded. It is also true that Antoine was a willing participant in the Indian slave trade. One has to put these facts in the perspective of the period, however. America itself was a slave holding nation. To many easterners coming west during those years, most Indians were counted as less than human. Antoine Robidoux was probably no different than others in his profession. Success often meant being willing and able to adapt to local circumstances, and he fit that definition well.

If Antoine had one defining trait, it was his relationship with the western wilderness. Within months of having built Fort Uncompahgre, he was deep in the Utah mountains leading a trapping expedition, content to leave management of the new trading post to his brother Louis.

His Santa Fe business affairs were often in the hands of various brothers or close friends. When supplies needed transport from Santa Fe to the outlying trading posts, it was often Antoine who made the trip.

While he and his wife Carmel left no children of their own, they did adopt an orphan girl from the Santa Fe region named Marina Anaya. The Robidouxs called her Carmelette, Spanish for "Little Carmel." A few years after moving to Saint Joseph with her mother, Carmelette married a successful French/American trader named Isadore Barada. She died shortly after the birth of their first child in 1852. Antoine and Carmel adopted the baby, Amanda Marie.

Eight years later, following her husband's death, Carmel and her granddaughter returned to Santa Fe where they still owned the home purchased during the heyday of the family fur trading empire. Still considered part of the old upper class, Carmel saw to it that Amanda received an education both in the social and intellectual graces of the day. Vivacious and beautiful, much as her adopted grandmother had been before her, the young woman, after a proper courtship, wed a young German immigrant named Christian Stollsteimer. It proved a good marriage. Stollsteimer became one of early southwestern Colorado's most influential pioneers, eventually settling in the country that was once part of Antoine's vast trading empire. The Stollsteimer name can be found today on several landmarks, including a creek and a mesa south of the San Juan Mountains.

Following Amanda's marriage, Carmel moved with the young couple to the San Luis Valley where she was able to continue her long-time friendship with Kit Carson and his wife, the former then serving as commanding officer at nearby Fort Garland. The respected matriarch of the family, Carmel helped raise her eight great-grandchildren, teaching them Spanish, French and English. From their father they learned German and part of the Ute tongue, but Spanish remained the language of the home. In 1879 Amanda sold her Santa Fe property to L. Brandford Prince, Territorial Supreme Court Justice of New Mexico and later governor of the state. The home still stands today. Finally, in

Fort interpretor and guide Ed Maddox demonstrates the art of flint knapping. Nationally known for this skill, Maddox is also an expert in the old Ute method of brain tanning animal skins.

Courtesy *San Juan Silver Stage*

1888, at the age of seventy six, Carmel died on the Stollsteimer ranch near Durango, Colorado. The *Durango Morning Herald* wrote that she "...was known to be a lady of high Christian character and a true friend. Though she had outlived her allotted time, she leaves those who sincerely mourn her loss...."

Amanda, following the deaths of a son and her husband in 1906, sold the family properties and moved to Pasadena, California where she died in 1916. Several of her sons and daughters remained in Colorado, and Stollsteimer descendants can be found today in the Uncompahgre Valley living a few miles from the site of old Fort Uncompahgre. The story has been handed down that Carmel had kept a diary which she gave to Amanda, who then continued her own record of family happenings. Stollsteimer family members believe that the two diaries passed out of family hands and might still exist somewhere in California. So far, efforts made to track them down have proven fruitless. If located, Carmel's diary might very well answer questions about her husband and what happened that fateful autumn in 1844 when his trading empire on the western slope came crashing to an end. Unfortunately, none of the Robidoux brothers kept a diary and only fragmentary knowledge can be gained from various government records.

However, there are a few that deal with the years after 1844. The first known written record regarding the ruins of Fort Uncompahgre comes from the records of Captain John Gunnison's expedition of 1853. The Gunnison party, hoping to locate a transcontinental railroad route directly through the Rocky Mountains, had followed Antoine's old trail from the San Luis Valley to the site of the fort. Expedition journalist Lieutenant E. G. Beckwith wrote that the party met several small family groups of Utes near present day Montrose and that at first, they seemed terrified of the white soldiers. Finally, after having been been convinced that the survey party meant them no harm, more Indians began to appear. Beckwith recorded that most of the Utes were poorly dressed and that many of the elderly appeared in poor health. One woman rode in close enough for a good look at the soldiers. Behind her, on the same horse, sat four dirty, ragged and wide-eyed children. A Ute chief joined Gunnison's men and rode with them to their next campsite three miles south of Delta. The old warrior spoke fondly of having known Antoine Robidoux years earlier. The next morning, September 17, 1853, joined by several more Ute leaders, Gunnison handed out presents, and the warriors then led him past the remains of Fort Uncompahgre, which Beckwith described as "now entirely fallen to ruins". The party crossed the Gunnison River roughly a mile below the fort and continued north paralleling Highway 50 towards Grand Junction. A few days later, Gunnison and several of his party were killed by hostile Indians in Utah.

The next mention came from Captain R. B. Marcy who traveled from Fort Bridger to the San Luis Valley in December of 1857. He and his soldiers made camp near the ruins of Fort Uncompahgre which Marcy noted as having been burned. More poignantly, the captain described the Utes he met living near the ruins as a "ragged, villainous looking set" who flocked around the troops trying to steal anything that took their fancy. It had been more than thirteen years since the Ute people of the valley had been able to trade their skins and furs for Antoine's trade goods. Their standard of living had seriously declined.

Early homesteaders left oral traditions regarding the remains of an old fort below the confluence of the Uncompahgre and Gunnison Rivers. As the years passed and time destroyed the evidence, even the exact location came into question. Some believe it was early settlers who scavenged what remained for their own building purposes, thus destroying the ruins. One unsubstantiated story refers to adobe blocks having been salvaged and used by an early homesteader south of the site. This might have been possible providing the area had not been flooded out prior to the 1880s. Extensive search efforts in the late twentieth century have yielded nothing more than a continuing controversy about the location, although most searchers agree the site is approximately two miles below the confluences of the two rivers. Occasionally, artifacts have been found that some researchers relate to the fort. The area was also a favorite camping ground and one of the few local crossing points for the Gunnison, so these finds could just as easily relate to early mountain men, Utes or other travelers passing through.

The most plausible explanation is that the original fort site no longer exists. Aerial photographs show that the Gunnison River has changed course numerous times in the past 100 years or so—the most recent being from severe floods that occurred in 1914 and 1915. These dramatically changed the course of the river below the town of Delta and exactly in the area where the fort is thought to have stood. However it is possible that subsurface remains and artifacts might still lie hidden beneath river mud. Archeologists and local historians hold to the hope that someday Fort Uncompahgre's original site will be revealed.

Regarding Fort Uintah, Freemont, on hearsay, wrote in his journal that the post had been attacked and taken by Ute Indians after his 1844 visit and that its owner had been absent. He mentioned nothing more, but early settlers spoke of seeing a burned out area they assumed to be the ruins. Located on Northern Ute tribal lands, the presumed site is closed to the public.

Fort Robidoux, the third trading post, located somewhere along the junction of the Green and White Rivers has almost no mention beyond that of Antoine's own inscription on a sandstone rock regarding his intention to build it. Several historians have advanced the idea that it never consisted of anything more than a temporary trading camp, which was abandoned after Antoine ended local competition from Hudson Bay people. Supposedly, Ute historians know the exact site, but if this is true, such knowledge remains confidential.

Although the physical remains of Antoine Robidoux's empire are lost, the stories of those early days were not. One Delta County native, fascinated since boyhood with stories of Fort Uncompahgre, collected everything he could in regards to historical information and began approaching individuals within the Delta community about rebuilding the trading post. Finally, in early 1989, William M. Bailey and a cadre of supporters approached the Delta City Council about building a new Fort Uncompahgre up river from the original, on city land and within the boundaries of what was to become Confluence Park. It would be no small undertaking, but Bailey's plan was unique and the project was approved. A site was selected on an old landfill on the south bank of the Gunnison River and construction began, not with tax money or professional builders, but with donated materials and volunteer labor. The city agreed to take over the sponsorship and financial obligations of the fort following its completion.

Within weeks the first cabin had been built and walls were up for a second. More volunteers joined in and on June 30, 1990, most of the structures were in place and the new fort was opened to the public. Bailey, who sparked the dream and oversaw much of the construction, stayed on for the first month as director but then stepped down to pursue a career in rebuilding and restoring other historic sites and buildings in Colorado and surrounding states.

Fur traders had to be able to negotiate trades that were satisfactory both to themselves and their customers. Ute trappers and their wives quickly became very sophisticated regarding what products they wanted, Dan Deuter, director of the reconstructed Fort Uncompahgre, carries many of the items that were available more than a century-and-a-half ago.
Courtesy *Delta County Independent*

Dan Deuter, construction volunteer, internationally known western artist and historian, stepped into the directorship. Two months later he was joined by Ed Maddox—another volunteer, professional trapper, history buff and a master flint knapper capable of reproducing museum quality arrowheads and other stone tools. The fort was open March through mid-December that year. The two interpreters began tours for the general public and local school children, all the while continuing with various construction projects and surrounding the post with a high fence made from cottonwood pickets. Inmates from the nearby Delta Correctional Facility worked side by side with local citizens to complete this latest effort.

A small flock of rare Churro sheep, descendants of animals brought to New Mexico 400 years ago, took up residence at the fort. Chickens, similar to what would have once roamed the grounds, were allowed to do so again. Horses inhabit the corrals behind the post, and a dedicated cadre of volunteers and workers from the correctional facility continue with various projects and repairs. It is estimated that by 1998, more than 500 individuals have provided in excess of 5,000 hours of labor.

As word of the reconstruction of the fort began to spread, more visitors came. Schools from across western Colorado began annual trips for different student groups, particularly fourth graders studying Colorado history. The two-man staff, with the support of volunteer interpreters and a Board of Historical Authenticity, began offering overnight encampments and training seminars for adults—teaching skills that were common during the fur trade. Students learn how to remove the hair from deer hides and turn them into soft, pliable buckskin. Others fire and use the old fashioned adobe forge to make simple but practical iron and steel tools vital to that long-ago time. Cooking lessons are given and bread is baked in the massive *horno*, a mud oven similar to those found in Santa Fe and Mexico.

Even romance found its way into the schedule. Director Deuter and volunteer Ellie Kelso were married in front of the new trade room on a cold, sunny day in November, 1991. Surrounded by a crowd of friends, family and well wishers, many of whom had shared in the fort's reconstruction, the couple took their vows dressed in authentic replicas of clothing of the 1840s. The fort has continued to prove popular for frontier-type weddings and family gatherings of groups who have historical links to the Delta area. Two television documentaries have been filmed at the fort, and western artists make frequent use of the grounds

The reconstructed Fort Uncompahgre of today reflects very closely the construction of the original which was a collection of log buildings with dirt roofs surrounded by a flimsy perimeter fence of wooden pickets.
Courtesy *Delta County Independent*

and buildings. The guest book contains signatures of visitors all around the world. Members of the large Robidoux family, spread from Canada to Hawaii and now spelling their name more than forty different ways, have also toured the fort. Western historians visit regularly, intrigued partly by the furnishings, some of which date back to the time period of the fort itself. Bit by bit, written material is being collected relating to the first fort. It comes from books, manuscripts, photocopies of maps, diary excerpts and stories—all information giving a clearer picture of the years from 1828 until 1844, when this log and mud structure was familiar to nearly everyone who roamed western Colorado. Perhaps, based on its own unique beginning and the fact it is a living- history museum, the new fort might someday achieve a similar reputation.

During the trapping months, hours before the first visitors arrive, fort personnel drive to nearby sites to check traps. Although beaver were almost completely trapped out during the 1800s, recent years have seen a resurgence of the big rodents, so many that it has been necessary to keep their numbers in check to prevent damage to local irrigation canals and the large numbers of trees lining Delta County waterways. In one night, an adult beaver can cut down as many as seven trees of respectable size. When officials and private land owners determine a problem exists, fort trappers are called. Today, the traps used are high tech and far more humane. Visitors can see the animals skinned, the hides cleaned, stretched and dried, just as they were a century-and-a-half ago. Many of the pelts are sent to museums around the country for display purposes. A few people have voiced criticism of the program, desiring instead to see surplus beaver live-trapped and moved to other areas. They are not aware that beaver have returned to nearly all their original western ranges and are extremely territorial. Established adults will attack and attempt to kill new animals released within the former's home ground.

As the fort ages, new facts and probabilities are emerging. Already the first picket fence is rotting away below ground level. Roofs and other parts of the buildings are showing decay as well. In this modern day when treated posts and lumber are taken for granted, it is easy to forget how quickly natural cottonwood and pine decay. Although the original fort was undoubtedly built very similarly to the current reconstruction, it would also have gone through the same process. Within a few years, adequate replacement materials would have no longer been available near the fort site—gone, because trees suitable for construction would already have been cut down and used. A structure the size of Fort Uncompahgre would also have gone through incredible amounts of firewood both for heating and cooking. This would suggest the fort might have gradually metamorphosed towards the use of another building material—adobe mud bricks.

Nearly all trading posts of record in early Colorado were made of this building material. Bent's Fort, located in southeastern Colorado along a river similar to the Gunnison, was constructed of adobe by workers brought up from Santa Fe and Taos. So were the string of posts located north of Denver along the South Platte River; Forts Lupton, Vasquez, Jackson, and Saint Vrain were all documented as having been of adobe construction. El Pueblo, from which the present city takes its name, was another example. All these forts were located along rivers with conditions similar to those encountered in the region where Fort Uncompahgre was constructed. Written accounts by those who visited the original fort say nothing about it being any different. Had construction remained entirely of wood, it is probable that this fact would have been recorded since that would have been a departure from the norm.

The frustrating point is that no one wrote much of anything about the fort, particularly in its later years. In addition, if adobe had been used, once the post was abandoned and the roofs caved in or burned, the walls—being exposed to rain, snow and floods—would have soon disappeared leaving little or no trace of the original structures other than possible traces of the foundations. Numerous western military posts built of adobe met this fate. While logic and observation support the idea of adobe construction, hard facts have yet to be discovered that would give adequate support. Until and unless that proof someday surfaces, the adobe issue remains as conjecture and supposition.

Meanwhile the reconstructed fort serves the purpose of taking visitors beyond the museum experience, the revisionism of many modern historians and the romantic notions of western novelists. It provides an opportunity to see, touch and experience the early fur trading period. For the visionaries and volunteers who helped build it, that was the intent. ✦

Bibliography

Alter, J. Cecil. "Old Trails, Old Forts, Old Trappers and Traders,"
Utah Historical Quarterly. Vol. IX, 1941.

Barton, John D. *Antoine Robidoux And The Fur Trade Of The Uinta Basin
1824-1844.* Vernal, Utah: Oakfield Publishing Company, 1996.

Chittenden, Hiran Martin. *The American Fur Trade of the Far West.*
Vol. I. Lincoln, Nebraska: University of Nebraska Press, 1986.

_____. *The American Fur Trade of the Far West. Vol. II.* Lincoln,
Nebraska: University of Nebraska Press, 1986.

Cleland, Robert Glass. *This Reckless Breed of Men.* New York,
New York: Alfred Knopf, 1950.

Cragin Collection. Colorado Springs Pioneers Museum.
Colorado Springs, Colorado.

Deuter, Dan. Private collection of miscellaneous material on
Fort Uncompahgre and Antoine Robidoux.
Fort Uncompahgre, Colorado.

Fort Uncompahgre File. Delta County Historical Society Museum.
Delta, Colorado.

Gowans, Fred R. *Rocky Mountain Rendezvous.* Layton, Utah:
Gibs M. Smith, Inc., 1985.

Gregg, Josiah. *Commerce of the Prairies.* Edited by Max L. Moorhead.
Norman, Oklahoma: University of Oklahoma Press, 1954.

Hafen, LeRoy R. "Fort Davy Crockett, Its Fur Men and Visitors,"
The Colorado Magazine. Denver, Colorado, January, 1952.

_____. *Mountain Men and Fur Traders of the Far West.* Lincoln, Nebraska: University of Nebraska Press, 1982.

_____. *The Mountain Men and the Fur Trade of the Far West. Vol. IV.* Glendale, California: Arthur H. Clark, 1966.

Hafen, Leroy R. & Hafen, Ann W. *Old Spanish Trail.* Lincoln, Nebraska: University of Nebraska Press, 1993.

Hill, Joseph J. "Antoine Robidoux, Kingpin in the Colorado Fur Trade, 1824-1844," *The Colorado Magazine.* Denver, Colorado, July, 1930.

Lecompte, Janet. *Pueblo-Hardscrabble-Greenhorn.* Norman, Oklahoma: University of Oklahoma Press, 1978.

Maddox, Debbie. "Life At Fort Uncompahgre," Unpublished paper. Montrose, Colorado, 1992.

Marsh, Charles S. *People Of The Shining Mountains.* Boulder, Colorado: Pruett Publishing Company, 1982.

Mattes, Merrill J. "Joseph Robidoux's Family," *Overland Journal. Vol. VI.* No. 3. Oregon, California Trail Assn., 1988.

"The Museum Of The Fur Trade Quarterly" Chadron, Nebraska: Assorted Issues from 1966 to 1995.

The Palace of the Governors-Museum of New Mexico, Santa Fe, New Mexico.

Pettit, Jan. *Utes, The Mountain People.* Colorado Springs, Colorado: Century One Press, 1982.

Rabideau, Clyde M. *The Robidous In North America 350 Years 1643-1993.* (Private Printing), 1993.

Reagan, Albert B. "Forts Robidoux and Kit Carson in Northeastern Utah," *New Mexico Historical Review,* April 1935.

Richardson, Wanda. "Antoine Robidoux," Unpublished paper. Uintah County, Utah.

Roberts, Jack. "Fort Robidoux," Unpublished paper. Redstone, Colorado, 1975.

Robidoux, Orral (Messmore). *Memorial to the Robidoux Brothers.* Smith-Grieves Co., 1924.

Ross, David. "The Battle of San Pasqual," *Ramona Magazine,* December 1994.

Ruxton, George F. *Life In The Far West.* Norman, Oklahoma: University of Oklahoma Press, 1951.

Saint Joseph Historical Society, Robidoux Row, Saint Joseph, Missouri.

"San Pasqual Battlefield State Historic Park Guide Book," California Department of Parks and Recreation.

Vandenbusche, Duane & Smith, Duane A. *A Land Alone: Colorado's Western Slope.* Boulder, Colorado: Pruett Publishing Company, 1981.

Victor, Frances F. *The River Of The West. Vol. I. Edited by Winfred Blevins. Missoula, Montana:* Mountain Press Publishing Company, 1983.

Wallace, William S. *Antoine Robidoux 1794-1860: A Biography of A Western Venturer.* Glen Dawson, 1953.

Weber, David J. *The Taos Trappers: The Fur Trade in the Southwest, 1540-1846.* Norman, Oklahoma: University of Oklahoma Press, 1971.